WILD swimming
Walks

NORTH DEVON AND EXMOOR
28 coast, river & waterfall days out

Sophie Pierce and Matt Newbury

WILD
THINGS
PUBLISHING

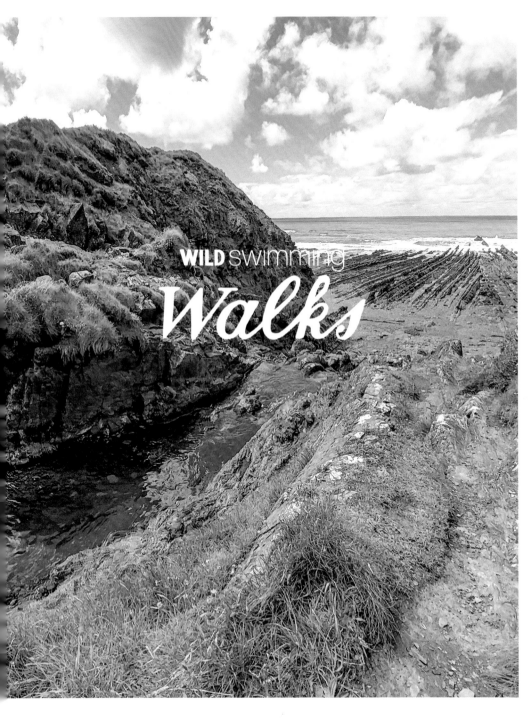

WILD swimming
Walks

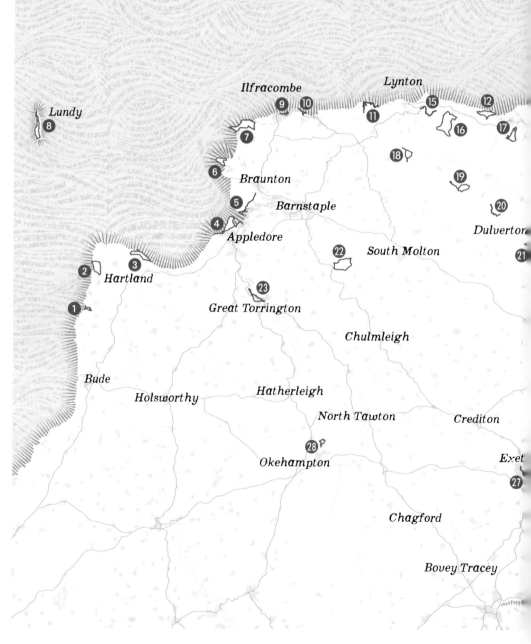

Lundy

Ilfracombe

Lynton

Braunton

Barnstaple

Appledore

Hartland

Great Torrington

South Molton

Dulverton

Chulmleigh

Bude

Holsworthy

Hatherleigh

North Tawton

Crediton

Okehampton

Exet

Chagford

Bovey Tracey

THE WALKS

Page

01. Welcombe Mouth and Marsland Circular 27
02. Hartland Quay and Speke's Mill Mouth Circular 33
03. Blackchurch Rock and Clovelly Circular 39
04. Appledore and Westward Ho! 47
05. Velator Quay and Crow Point 53
06. Baggy Point and Caves 59
07. Mortehoe Circular 65
08. Lundy 71
09. Ilfracombe and Hele Bay Circular 77
10. Watermouth and Broadsands 83
11. Heddon's Mouth and Woody Bay 89
12. Porlock Weir and Culbone Church 95
13. Dunster Circular 99
14. East Quantoxhead and St Audrie's Bay 107
15. East Lyn Adventure 113
16. Badgworthy Water Circular 119
17. Horner Water circular 127
18. Pinkery Pond 133
19. Landacre Bridge and Cow Castle 139
20. Tarr Steps and River Barle Circular 145
21. Dulverton and Exebridge 151
22. The Taw Tumble 159
23. River Torridge and Torrington Commons 167
24. Taunton Circular 173
25. Tiverton Figure of Eight 179
26. Killerton and the River Culm 185
27. Exeter and the River Exe 191
28. Abbeyford Woods and East Okement River 199

TABLE OF WALKS

No.	NAME	SWIMMING TYPE
1	Welcombe Mouth and Marsland Circular	Sea and waterfall pools
2	Hartland Quay and Speke's Mill Mouth Circular	Sea and waterfall pools
3	Blackchurch Rock and Clovelly Circular	Sea at Clovelly and Mouthmill
4	Appledore and Westward Ho!	Sea and tidal pools
5	Velator Quay and Crow Point	Sea at Crow Point; tidal river at Velator Quay
6	Baggy Point and Caves	Sea, rock pool, gullies and cave
7	Mortehoe Circular	Sea at Lee Bay, Bennett's Mouth and Grunta Beach
8	Lundy	Sea at the Landing Place and other locations
9	Ilfracombe and Hele Bay Circular	Sea at Rapparee Cove and Hele Bay
10	Watermouth and Broadsands	Sea at Watermouth Bay and Broadsands
11	Heddon's Mouth and Woody Bay	Sea at Heddon's Mouth and Woody Bay
12	Porlock Weir and Culbone Church	Sea at Porlock Weir
13	Dunster Circular	Sea at Blue Anchor Beach
14	East Quantoxhead and St Audrie's Bay	Sea at Kilve Beach and St Audrie's Bay
15	East Lyn Adventure	Pools in the East Lyn River
16	Badgworthy Water Circular	Pools in Badgworthy Water
17	Horner Water Circular	Pool in River Horner
18	Pinkery Pond	Moorland lake
19	Landacre and Cow Castle	Pools in River Barle
20	Tarr Steps and River Barle Circular	Pools in River Barle
21	Dulverton and Exebridge	Pools in River Barle and Exe
22	The Taw Tumble	Pools in the River Taw
23	River Torridge and Torrington Commons	Pools in River Torridge
24	Taunton Circular	Pools in River Tone
25	Tiverton Figure of Eight	Pools in River Exe
26	Killerton and the River Culm	Pools in River Culm
27	Exeter and the River Exe	Pools in River Exe
28	Abbeyford Woods and East Okement River	Pools in River Okement

TERRAIN	REFRESHMENTS	MILES	DIFFICULTY
Coast path and steep hills	None	3 miles	Medium
Coast path and steep hills	Hotel/pub in Hartland	4 miles	Medium
Coast path and steep hills	Cafés in Clovelly	6 miles	Hard
Coast path	Cafés in Westward Ho! and Appledore	7/8 miles	Medium
Mostly flat walking	None on route; cafés in Braunton	6 miles	Medium
Coast path, rough ground, gentle hills	Cafés and pubs in Croyde	4 miles	Medium
Coast path and numerous steep hills	Cafés and pubs in Mortehoe	8 miles	Hard
One steep hill, rough paths	Pub on Lundy	3 miles	Medium
Coast path and hills	Cafés in Ilfracombe and Hele Bay	3 miles	Medium
Coast path and steep hills	Café in Watermouth Bay	3 miles	Medium
Coast path and very steep climbs	Café at Hunters Inn	8 miles	Hard
Steep hills, woodland paths	Cafés at Porlock Weir	6 miles	Hard
Steep hills and coast path	Cafés and pubs in Dunster	6.5 miles	Hard
Coast path; tracks, some ascents	None	6 miles	Medium
Riverside walking, some hills	Café at Watersmeet	5.5 miles	Medium
Steep climbs, rough ground	Tea room at Malmsmead	8 miles	Hard
One steep hill, rough paths	Café at Horner	6 miles	Medium
Rough ground, some hills	None	4 miles	Medium
Rough tracks and paths; gentle hills	None	6 miles	Medium
Mostly flat, some rough ground	Pub at Tarr Steps	4 miles	Medium
Riverside walking, some hills	Cafés and pubs in Dulverton and Exebridge	4.5 miles	Medium
Some hills and rough paths	Pub at Chittlehampton	6 miles	Medium
Some hills, rough ground	Cafés en route and in Torrington	5 miles	Medium
Mostly flat walking	Cafés and pubs in Taunton	3 miles	Easy
Mostly flat walking	Cafés and pubs in Tiverton	5 miles	Medium
Woodland tracks and gentle hills	Cafés at Killerton	4 miles	Medium
Flat riverside walking	Cafés and pubs in Exeter	4 miles	Easy
Some ascent; woodland paths	None on route; cafés in Okehampton	3 miles	Easy

Porlock Weir

INTRODUCTION

What a sea-wall they are, those Exmoor hills! Sheer upward from the sea a thousand feet…

Charles Kingsley, Prose Idylls

A swim at Porlock Weir in Somerset perfectly illustrates what is so magical about coastal Exmoor. You are surrounded by vast, dramatic scenery: over to the east is the enormous, dominant headland of Hurlstone Point, while to the south the coast is notably wooded – Exmoor has the most extensive broadleaved coastal woods in Britain. This tiny harbour has been here for centuries and feels quiet and tucked away, like many of the communities in this part of the West Country. The main channel is still marked by simple wooden sticks called withies, and right next to the water, a small area called Turkey Island has a picturesque row of ancient thatched and tiled cottages. There is both grandeur and intimacy here, a memorable combination.

Inland, another flavour of the magnificent variety here is found on the short journey from the village of Simonsbath, in the heart of moorland Exmoor, north to Watersmeet and then on to Lynmouth on the coast. As you leave the village and ascend to Brendon Common, you feel the immense isolation and grandeur of the moorland, which stretches almost to the sea. You see tiny river valleys etched into the landscape, where the hillsides fold around the slivers of water. As you approach Watersmeet, you get a grand view of the ocean unlike any other: two huge sections of distant blue with an enormous triangular headland looming up in the middle, dividing the sea like some sort of monster rising from the depths. This is Foreland Point – known locally simply as 'The Foreland' in recognition of its vastness – an immense, pointed promontory with sheer cliffs dropping down to the water. It shelters the eastern part of the coast, which is why these cliffs are so extensively wooded. The view disappears as you descend into the steep, dramatic valleys of the East Lyn River, which have such an alpine feel that the Victorians named the area 'Little Switzerland'. The many different environments of this one brief journey make Exmoor so special; the sheer variety of landscapes in a relatively small area, all somehow feeling intimately connected.

This part of the world is known for its 'hogsback' cliffs – great shoulders of rock that drop dramatically to the sea. It has the highest coastline on the British mainland, reaching 314 metres at Culbone Hill. The Exmoor shoreline is also the most remote in England; there is no access by land to large stretches of it, and even with a boat there are many places that are completely inaccessible. Many of the walks in this book are pretty challenging, because of the steep climbs and descents: the coast path through Somerset and on to Devon is like a rollercoaster at times. But by the same token, the views are impressive and rewarding, from the towering headlands at Hurlstone Point to the red cliffs at Woody Bay, the vast sand dunes at Braunton Burrows and the broken, contorted rocks of Hartland, which the Romans called the 'Promontory of Hercules'.

This coastline contains all manner of different swim experiences. In the most easterly part, a fossil-filled stone pavement forms the seabed and ridges of rock edge the shore at Kilve on the Somerset coast. Heading west, you reach Blue Anchor Bay, a huge beach which is only swimmable at high tide; still further west, the tiny

Spekes Mill Mouth

Coast path near Woody Bay

harbour and shingle of Porlock Weir is a complete contrast. Heading into Devon, at Watermouth you can swim around Sexton's Burrow, a half-tidal island sitting at the mouth of the cove. Hele Bay, just next to Ilfracombe, has a handy slipway into the water and is sheltered, making it beloved by a big local community of swimmers. Heading down to Baggy Point, you will find an enchanting lagoon on the southern edge of the headland, while Velator Quay at the mouth of the Taw-Torridge estuary is a beautiful tidal river swim off an elegant wooden jetty. The most south-westerly part of the coast in the book, from Bideford to Marsland Mouth, has fantastical rock formations and several huge waterfalls crashing down onto the beaches below. These coastal waterfalls are a feature of this part of the British coast, but rare elsewhere; the only other place they are found in Europe is in the fjords of Norway.

Exmoor is quieter and less showy than its famous neighbour, Dartmoor. It is lower – its highest point is Dunkery Beacon, at 519 metres – and smaller, at 267 square miles. It has a more intimate feel – although it retains a rugged bleakness on the wilder, more exposed expanses. There are several areas of ancient woodland, as well as many charming villages and towns in a predominantly agricultural landscape away from the moor. Its rivers are mostly quite small; the largest is the Barle which rises high on the central moorlands and joins the River Exe at Exebridge. From here the Exe gets progressively bigger as it makes its way to the sea at Exmouth. The book contains swims in both the Barle and the Exe, as well as in smaller watercourses including the East Lyn River and Horner Water. Further south-west, into the districts of North and Mid-Devon and Torridge, lie the great tidal rivers the Taw and the Torridge, but many of the other rivers are quite small and not so good for swimming.

The Victorians loved Exmoor and were responsible for creating many of the features we see today.

River Barle near Dulverton

Tourists were coming as early as the 1820s; in 1823 work started on creating Tunnels Beaches in Ilfracombe, with hundreds of Welsh miners employed to hack tunnels through the cliffs so that people could get to the beaches. Some of their pick-axe marks are still visible on the walls of the tunnels today. Then, three tidal pools were built – two for the ladies and one for the gentlemen; one of them has survived to this day and is well worth a visit.

Tourism took off in earnest when the North Devon Railway Company started operating to Barnstaple and then Bideford in the 1850s; the line was extended to Ilfracombe in the 1870s. Landowners and entrepreneurs saw the potential of the dramatic scenery and set about finding ways of getting the public there. In 1890 the Lynton and Lynmouth Cliff Railway opened, and in 1893 enterprising businessman Benjamin Lake built a road down to Woody Bay, where he also created a tidal swimming pool and a small quay. If not for him, there is no way we would be able to reach this beautiful beach today.

Appledore

Horner Wood

The RD Blackmore novel *Lorna Doone*, which was published in 1869, has also been bringing tourists to the area for over 150 years. Subtitled *A Romance of Exmoor*, it is a love story packed with equal parts melodrama and vivid descriptions of the countryside in and around the valley of Badgworthy Water (the Valley of the Doones). Although the novel is probably not to most modern readers' tastes, the Lorna Doone story is still heavily promoted by local tourism organisations.

Others inspired by the landscape of Exmoor and North Devon include Henry Williamson, author of *Tarka the Otter* and himself a keen open-water swimmer. Charles Kingsley's book *Westward Ho!* was so popular that it led to the creation of a seaside resort named after it, where Rudyard Kipling went to school. The allure and wildness of the scenery also inspired poets including Wordsworth, Coleridge and Shelley.

Today, people enjoy the coast and countryside of Exmoor and North Devon for the same reasons they always have – for their beauty, drama, and peace. There is a growing awareness of the fragility of our wild environments, and a large part of North Devon is designated an UNESCO biosphere, one of only seven in the UK. The area includes all of the coast, Lundy Island and the sea

around it, and a huge area inland extending from Okehampton in the south to near Tiverton in the east, taking in a whole variety of places including Hatherleigh, South Molton, and Torrington.

It has been designated for its outstanding natural features. At the shore these include dramatic coastal landscapes, one of the best dune systems in the northern hemisphere, and flagship marine species from dolphins and seals to pink sea fans. Inland, the designation recognises iconic river fauna such as otters and salmon, the blanket bogs of Exmoor, western oak woodlands supporting a multitude of pollution-sensitive lichens, and landscape characteristics such as culm grasslands and Devon hedgerows.

The purpose of UNESCO biospheres is to be 'learning places for sustainable development', finding ways to reconcile the conservation of biodiversity with its sustainable use. In North Devon, the biosphere acts as a test-bed for sustainable development in an area of world-class natural value: many projects are in progress, including the control of invasive species such as Himalayan balsam and Japanese knotweed, the management of fisheries to ensure sustainable catches, a programme to use the natural environment to improve public health, and a scheme to develop local supply chains for the green economy.

anding jetty at Lundy Island

Steps at Kilve Beach

er Park Pool, Badgworthy Water

Blackchurch Rock, Mouthmill Beach

THE SCOPE OF THIS BOOK

Although the book's title is Exmoor and North Devon, we have included locations down as far as the A30 and M5. This is because many swimmers live in several places on its edge – including Taunton, Exeter and Okehampton – and look to Exmoor and the north Devon coast for adventures. These locations are also not currently in any other swimming books, so we felt it important to include them. You will notice that the vast majority of swims are on the north coast; inland river swims are hard to find, because many of the rivers are small and there is a lack of public footpaths running alongside. There is a big hole in the middle of our swim map for this book, around South Molton, Chulmleigh and Witheridge; we have failed to find any decent swim spots in this area; please let us know if you know of any!

TIDES AND WEATHER CONDITIONS FOR EXMOOR AND NORTH DEVON

For this part of the coast, when is just as important as where you swim. The Bristol Channel has the highest tidal range in all of Europe and the second highest in the world, second only to the Bay of Fundy in Canada. This means that in many places swimming is only possible at high tide; at low water the tide is simply too far out. We provide detailed instructions about timings for many of the swim walks in this book, because if you go at the wrong time, you may well find there is no water to swim in! One rather lovely side-effect of this is the growth of unusually strong communities of swimmers. Why? Well, if you can only swim at high water, lots of people inevitably converge on the beach at the same time, rather than coming and going throughout the day and missing each other in the process.

Always make sure you know what the tide is doing before you set off. You can buy tide tables in many local shops, including newsagents, garages, convenience stores and bookshops. These give the whole year's times; you can also check online or use a free tide app, but the times given on these are only for the next seven days. If you want the whole year, you have to pay a few pounds.

It is important to understand the difference between 'spring' and 'neap' tides. A spring tide (which is nothing to do with the season of spring), occurs around the time of the full and new moons when the combined pull of the sun and moon moves far more water around. So the tide comes in and goes out much further than on a neap, when the difference between high and low water is at its smallest. Your tide table will tell you when they are, and you can use them to your advantage. For example, if you swim at low water on a spring tide, you might be able to see marine life that is normally hidden beneath the water, for example starfish and anemones. Similarly, when you know that the water will be deeper than normal at high water on a spring tide, you might go on a swim around some particularly interesting rocks or islands. If you're doing a challenging swim, perhaps around an island, you would be better off on a neap when there is less water moving around; it would also be a good idea to swim at 'slack water' which is the hour or so at the top or the bottom of the tide when the water is moving most slowly.

When planning a sea swim, it's also very useful to look at the wind forecast as well as the tides, to get an idea of how rough the sea might be. If you want calm water, you don't want the wind blowing from the sea onto the land, as this is likely to make the sea more turbulent. Many of the beaches on this stretch of coast face west, so ideally you would need an easterly wind or no wind at all. However, the prevailing winds in this part of the world are south-westerly, which is not a great help, so look at the wind speed; if it's below 10 knots/11.5mph there is a good chance of the sea being calm.

WILD SWIMMING SAFETY

*P*lan your walk, taking necessary supplies and protection; don't forget water, map, first aid kit, compass and waterproofs. Always establish an exit point before entering water, especially fast-flowing water. If you are unsure whether there's a current, swim out a short distance and then swim back to see if it feels any different. Take extra care following heavy rainfall, when rivers might be in spate and flowing much faster than normal.

Never jump or dive into water without first checking the depth and whether there are any obstructions. Even if you have jumped or dived there before, always check every time: large obstructions like tree branches and rocks move about underwater, and an area that was previously clear may well be blocked.

Swim in a group wherever possible; if swimming alone, let people know your movements and take extra care. Don't swim when you've been drinking alcohol. Wear a brightly coloured swim cap and use a tow float to help you be seen, especially if you are in an area with a lot of boats.

If swimming in the sea, always check the tide before you set out. Watch out in high surf: rip currents can form which take you out to sea, to the wrong side of the breaking waves. Swim at right angles to them to escape, then body-surf back in. Beware of tidal currents, especially near estuary mouths and around headlands, especially at mid-tide and on fortnightly spring tides, when flows are strongest.

If you are concerned about water quality, cover cuts and open wounds with plasters and do not swim front crawl.

Long Pool, East Lyn River

The River Okement at Abbeyford Woods

Life Rock, Hartland Quay

Pool in Strawberry Water above Welcombe Mouth

KEEPING WARM

All of our swim walks can be done all the year round, but remember that cold water can limit your swimming endurance. If it is your first outdoor swim of the season, be careful to enter the water slowly and acclimatise. Stay close to the shore until you are comfortable. Do not overestimate your ability. Remember that cold water quickly causes hypothermia – shivering is the first stage.

The more you swim, the more you acclimatise. Everyone has different levels of tolerance of the cold: you need to learn how much you can take and get out before you start to feel really cold. You lose a lot of heat through your head, so wear a swimming hat (this also helps you to be seen). Of course, wearing a wetsuit is always a good idea when it's cold, and there are brilliant wetsuits purpose-made for swimming rather than surfing. Wetsuit gloves and boots are also a great way to keep warm, if you don't yet want to wear a wetsuit but need some protection against the cold. In the colder months of the year, it's vital to take warm clothing, particularly a woolly hat and socks, to change into immediately afterwards.

SEA TEMPERATURES

We all know that the water is warmest in the summer, but not many people realise that it is still pretty warm in October, November and even December. Indeed, in these months the water tends to be warmer than in the early summer. The Centre for Environment, Fisheries and Aquaculture Science (CEFAS) collates sea temperature readings from all over the country on its website. Taking Ilfracombe as an example, readings taken over the last 30 years show that on average, January to March are the coldest months, at around 8°C. From April the temperature rises, peaking in August at around 16–17°C, double what it is in the first months of the year. It's still pretty warm through the autumn, at 14°C in October and around 12°C in November.

Seal on Lundy

SEALS

There are more than 120,000 grey seals around the coast of Britain – 40% of the world's population – and you may well encounter one when swimming in the seas off North Devon and Somerset. (Common seals are also seen, but far less frequently in the south-west.) They are curious creatures, rather like dogs, and might well approach you; it is best to swim away from them calmly and quietly, avoiding sudden movements. They are unlikely to hurt you but sometimes like to explore with their mouths, which can result in a bite. If this happens, seek medical advice as you may well need antibiotics. If swimming in an area where you know there are seals and you are worried, wear a wetsuit and gloves and boots so your body is protected.

The general rule is to stay away from seals, as they are wild animals and human interaction is stressful for them. Any disturbance, in the water or on land, threatens their survival. If you see a seal hauled out on a rock or the beach, do not approach it. Seals use enormous amounts of energy hunting, and need this time to rest.

Pupping season is between September and December, so be particularly careful to avoid seals at this time. If you see a pup on a beach, stay away from it; its parents will be nearby, even if you can't see them.

PRACTICALITIES

Ordnance Survey 1:25,000 Explorer maps are essential, and come both as traditional paper maps and as an app. You can also see OS mapping for free on a desktop computer at home using Bing maps, but this does not work on mobile phones or tablets. You can print these maps; some people make 'screen grabs' of the appropriate section and save them or email them for use later on their phones. We give detailed directions for all the walks and swims, doing our best to describe the route, but it's important to realise that you cannot rely on written directions alone, particularly for some of the more remote swims and walks. A map is vital, and a compass is also very useful.

Downloadable route information to print out or transfer to your smartphone can be found at wildthingspublishing.com/exmoor. Insert the last two words of each chapter introduction, with no spaces or capitals. For example, for Walk 1 go to wildthingspublishing.com/exmoor/journeyhome.

Brendon Common, Exmoor

Mermaids Pool, Baggy Point

Heddon Valley

Clovelly Harbour

Path near Heddons Mouth

River Torridge, Torrington

Grunta Beach

Bennett's Mouth near Mortehoe

RIGHTS AND RESPONSIBILITIES

The impact of leisure activities on wild places can be a heated issue, particularly since the pandemic, when more people than ever descended on the coast and countryside, unable to go to holiday destinations abroad or pursue their usual hobbies. Sadly, some people want to blame walkers and swimmers for increased littering in beauty spots, or claim that we have a negative effect on delicate ecosystems. It's true that certain places have become very popular in recent years; we all need to be aware of the potential impact we can have on the environment.

Walking to places, and not just visiting 'honeypots' where you can just drive up and swim, is a good start, and that is the whole philosophy of this book. It is so much more rewarding to walk to a swim spot, enjoying the outing and taking in the beauty of the countryside, than simply to 'swim and go'. It also helps to spread out the impact of visitors. We've created a wild swimmers' code, to be absolutely clear about the responsibilities we have to protecting wild places. It's common sense to all of us, but if we leave no trace and take away more litter than we came with, we are no longer open to accusations of environmental irresponsibility. We've also only included walks and swims that can be reached from public footpaths and access land; while we are real advocates for access to swim spots and walking routes, we don't want to escalate any existing tensions.

On that note, we've seen a growth in prohibition signs, banning us from doing everything from picnicking to swimming. Perhaps understandably, landowners have become fed up with people who do not respect the countryside, but of course this ends up penalising the majority who do care

about the environment and look after it. In particular, signs have gone up at some places where swimming has traditionally taken place for many years without any problem. If you encounter such signs, it is up to you to exercise your judgement as to whether you swim or not.

All of the information in this book was correct at the time of publication, but things do change all of the time. A landowner may decide not to allow swimming from the banks of their land, or a cliff fall may lead to a section of coast path being closed. If you come across any problems with any of the routes, let us know and we will update this on the website and in any future editions of this book.

THE WILD SWIMMING CODE

- Car-share whenever possible and park sensibly, not blocking roads, turning places or gateways.

- Do not leave litter, and pick up any rubbish that you find.

- Do nothing to damage the environment, and take all your rubbish away.

- Do not light fires, including disposable barbecues.

- Respect other water users, including anglers and canoeists/kayakers.

- Between November and January, take care not to tread in the gravel in freshwater rivers where fish such as trout and salmon lay their eggs.

- Leave only footprints, take only memories.

Spekes Mill Mouth

FINDING FELLOW SWIMMERS

There are lots of friendly groups on Facebook you can join to meet up with other swimmers:

• Baggy Bluetits
• Bluetits of Westward Ho!
• Devon Wild Swimming
• Hele Bay Merbabes
• Minehead Polar Bears
• North Devon Open Water Swimmers

Watermouth Bay

The Outdoor Swimming Society is a national organisation, but is another great place to find like-minded swimmers, information and organised events (www.outdoorswimmingsociety.com).

Porlock Weir

Walk 1

WELCOMBE AND MARSLAND

A short but strenuous walk in Devon's most westerly parish, taking in the wild and rugged Welcombe and Marsland valleys, with swims in both the sea and waterfalls.

INFORMATION

DISTANCE: 3 miles
TIME: Allow 3 hours
MAP: OS Explorer 126 Clovelly & Hartland
START AND END POINT: Welcombe Mouth car park (SS 212 180, EX39 6HJ, What3Words: books.observer.headers)
PUBLIC TRANSPORT: None
SWIMMING: Welcombe Mouth beach (SS 211 179) and waterfall (SS 212 180), Marsland Mouth beach (SS 212 174), and Strawberry Water waterfall (SS 213 181)
REFRESHMENTS: None on the walk so take supplies. The Old Smithy Inn is a gorgeous thatched pub with a lovely garden at the head of the Welcombe Valley (01288 331305, EX39 6HG)
EASIER ACCESS: The car park at Welcombe is right next to the beach, and if you go at high tide you avoid walking across the reef to get to the sea
NEARBY SWIM SPOTS: Stanbury Mouth just over the border in Cornwall is another wild and beautiful beach

rriving at Welcombe Mouth ❶ feels a bit like standing on the edge of the world. The sea stretches out from a beautifully remote spot at the end of what seems like an endless journey down tiny roads. A word of warning: the drive down to the car park is along a somewhat pot-holed track; it is perfectly doable in an ordinary car as long as you go slowly and carefully, but it's as well to be warned. The sea swims on this walk are best done in calm weather with little wind; when rollers are pounding the beach there is a risk you will be thrown against the rocks.

It's lovely to start the walk with a swim. At low tide it is a long walk to the water, picking your way between the rocky fingers which form a dramatic reef at right angles to the shoreline. The sand here moves around all the time, so on one day the walk might be quite easy, but on another there might be no sand, and you'll need to navigate the rocks. For optimum swimming, it's best to visit at high water – but on the other hand you then won't get as good a look at the rock formations, which are spectacular. Either way, by the time you get to the second swim spot at Marsland Mouth, the tide will have moved, so you will have a different experience swimming there.

The rocks here are part of the Crackington Formation, noted for the intense folding of sandstones and shales. The layers were created over 300 million years ago in the Carboniferous period and then compressed and contorted into the shapes we see today by tectonic events in the Devonian, an era named because it was first studied in this county. If you stand on the beach looking out to sea along the clefts in the rocks, and then turn to look the other way, you can see the same clefts continuing on up into the cliffs. Imagining the movements which caused them is quite something and can make you feel dizzy!

Before setting off on the walk, it's good to rinse off in the waterfall that you can find at the northern end of the beach, which is rather fun as it has two pools: an 'upstairs' and a 'downstairs'. You can either climb up to it from the shore, or walk to it from the car park over some stepping stones. The pools are only small, but enough to wash off the salt. There is another waterfall further upstream, which we'll come to later. Their presence here, as well as in other locations nearby like Speke's Mill Mouth, is all down to geology. The descending river valleys have been truncated by the eroding cliffline, so their floors lie above sea level. The rivers are unable to erode the hard rock, so end up falling to the sea as dramatic waterfalls.

The first part of the route involves ascending a very steep hill, a typical feature of this part of the North Devon scenery, packed as it is with precipitous combes. In summer the hedgerows along the path are laced with honeysuckle and other wild flowers. You cross a field and then start to descend towards Marsland Mouth, where you soon pass a small stone building with a slate roof, looking out to sea ❸. This is known as Ronald Duncan's Writing Hut, and is named after the man who built it on the site of an old coastguard's lookout.

Ronald Duncan was a poet, playwright, librettist, pacifist and farmer, who moved to West Mill in the Marsland Valley (which we will pass later in the walk) in 1937. He had visited the area as a child and had always wanted to move back. When he arrived with his soon-to-be-wife they lived a very basic existence: there was no electricity, they had to collect their water from the stream, and the only heating was open fires. When war broke out, Ronald Duncan invited other pacifists to come and

form a community, and they farmed the local area. Sadly, the experiment was not a success, and the community disbanded after a few years.

Duncan built the hut in the early 1960s and would go there every day to write; he composed one of his most famous works, an epic poem called *Man*, in the hut. In the third part of his autobiography, Obsessed, he describes the site. "The view attracted me because it contained no signs of humanity: the open Atlantic, the bracken and gorse covered cliffs, giant boulders on the beach beneath. The only signs of life were the buzzards and a single unmated falcon. I was drawn to this view which had not changed since the Cambrian era."

Despite being a prolific writer, who published numerous poems, plays, essays and libretti, Ronald Duncan is not that well known; perhaps because he spread himself across many different genres. The hut fell into disrepair after his death in 1982, but it was restored by his daughter Briony Lawson, who still owns West Mill (which can be rented out for holidays).

After signing the visitor's book in the hut, you continue to descend the path to Marsland Mouth, passing a footbridge over a stream – Marsland Water – which is the border between Devon and Cornwall. The southern half of the beach is actually in Cornwall, so this is the only beach which has the distinction of having a foot in each county!

Like Welcombe, Marsland Mouth ❹ is a riot of rock at low tide. Looking out to sea on the left-hand side, you will see a large triangular rock sticking out. This is called Gull Rock (one of many Gull Rocks all around the south-west coastline) and is popular with climbers; the locals call it the sleeping giant. An hour either side of low tide a lovely pool forms in the middle between here and Welcombe (main picture). It's a scramble to get to, but rather magical.

After another swim, the route takes you past West Mill ❺ and through a beautiful nature reserve that was originally owned by Christopher Cadbury, of the chocolate dynasty. It is now managed by the Devon Wildlife Trust, which describes it as "a magical, secretive mix of woodland, coastline and butterfly-filled meadows – all in a single stream valley". The area is an SSSI, and home to two rare British butterflies, the small pearl-bordered and pearl-bordered fritillaries. The woods have a variety of trees including ash, holly, rowan, beech, hazel and sycamore, and are home to dormice. The path passes a particularly beautiful spreading oak tree. (Please note that part of our route through the reserve is on a permissive path, which means that in theory it could be closed any time. Should that happen, you would need to carry straight on up the road from West Mill, from where you could pick up the rest of the route at point ❽.

After walking through the reserve, there's another strenuous climb up a winding rocky track ❼ which feels like a very ancient route, perhaps used by smugglers in centuries past. You emerge at the top of the hill again, and there is a short walk along a lane before you turn back towards the coast on a footpath. The route rejoins the path back down to Welcombe, with the walk downhill almost as challenging as when you climbed up. As you descend, you will get a great view of the stream running down to valley to the beach, which is called Strawberry Water. You will see a tempting waterfall a little way back from the coast, which you can visit after getting back to the car park. Dump all your stuff apart from swimming items in the car, and then take the path along the southern side of the stream (the car park side). Follow the water upstream and you will find a couple of places for a soothing dip to set you up for the journey home.

DIRECTIONS

1 From the car park, if you want to start with a swim, head straight down to the beach. To begin the walk, return to the car park and start up the road where you drove in. Turn immediately right onto the coast path, which is signed by a wooden post with an acorn and an oak leaf on it. Take the steep path to the top, passing a bench and then going over a wooden stile.
0.2 miles

2 Head straight past a stile on your left saying 'public footpath, Mead' – do not go left over stile. Walk across the field and then start a steep descent.
0.1 miles

3 You pass Ronald Duncan's Writing Hut on your right. Continue the descent. The path zig-zags and then bears left and you reach a metal gate on your left which leads inland. Do not go through, but turn sharply right towards the sea. Continue down past a footbridge over the stream on your left, and bear right to find the beach and second swim.
0.2 miles

4 From the beach retrace your steps back up the hill, as though going back to the hut, until you reach the metal gate. Go through the gate, walking towards the house ahead of you (West Mill).
0.3 miles

5 Pass West Mill on your right, and shortly after (where the road becomes concrete) take the path to the right.
0.2 miles

6 You reach a junction of paths, with a very small path on your immediate left, and a path bearing left uphill. Do not take either of these, but turn right through a wooden kissing gate next to a wooden five-bar gate. Once through the gate, turn left and walk along the left-hand side of the field. Keep left, and go through a wooden kissing gate at the end of the field on the left. Enter a wood, passing under a distinctive spreading oak tree, with a stream on your right.
0.3 miles

7 You reach a stony track. Turn left and follow the road as it bends uphill, passing a gate with a sign for the Devon Wildlife Trust on your right.
0.3 miles

8 You reach a road. Turn right here, continuing uphill and ignoring the public footpath sign pointing left. Pass Blueberry Hill house on your left and continue to a T-junction on a corner at the top of the hill. Turn left here (Mead Corner).
0.1 mile

9 Just after a sign on the left for Ley Park with a green letterbox, turn left off the road down a track, heading back towards the coast path. You reach a seven-bar metal gate with a stile beside it; cross the stile into a field and walk straight ahead on the right-hand side of the fields. You arrive back at the stile at point 2. Cross the stile, turn right and follow the path back down to the car park.
0.7 miles

HARTLAND QUAY AND SPEKES MILL MOUTH CIRCULAR

This spectacular hike from romantic Hartland Quay heads down the coast to the finest waterfall in North Devon, with swims in salt water and fresh, returning past historic St Nectan's Church. For best swimming, start as high tide approaches, and bring water shoes to protect your feet.

INFORMATION

DISTANCE: 4 miles
TIME: Allow 6 hours
MAP: OS Explorer 126 Clovelly and Hartland
START AND END POINT: Hartland Quay car park (SS 222 247, EX39 6DB What3Words: passages. manly.camera)
PUBLIC TRANSPORT: None to Hartland Quay; the nearest is the 219 bus from Bude to Hartland village
SWIMMING: Hartland Quay (SS 223 248), Childspit Beach (SS 223 242), Speke's Mill Mouth beach (SS 225 237) and waterfalls (SS 225 235), all best around high tide; at low water there are numerous rocks to navigate
REFRESHMENTS: The Hartland Quay Hotel has a wonderful position close to the water (01237 441218, EX39 6DU). Docton Mill Gardens and Tea Room is a very short diversion off the main walk route, open April to early October (01237 441369, EX39 6EA)
EASIER ACCESS: the car park at Hartland Quay is right next to the sea, with a slipway to the water that is also accessible to wheelchairs; you need to go at high tide to avoid walking across the reef to get to the sea
NEARBY SWIM SPOTS: Welcombe and Marsland Mouths; Blegberry Beach is a pebbly cove north of Hartland Quay

Hartland Quay ❶ teeters over the water on a promontory, in what must be one of the most beautiful settings along this piece of coast. Cliffs tower on one side, and the quay is surrounded by dramatic rocks protruding out of the water like sharks' fins. For the best swimming on this walk you need calm conditions and to set off around high tide; ideally, about an hour before. On rough days do be cautious – with big waves, there's a real risk of being thrown against the rocks.

However, if conditions are right, a dip is the perfect way to start the walk. On calm days the water is crystal clear, and it's fun to swim out to Life Rock just offshore, the only significant rock to still be visible at high water. Its name is a reference to this, because a shipwrecked sailor who managed to reach the rock had a chance of staying alive. On a sunny day it's a particular magnet for the youth, who like to jump off it from a great height.

As you move into the water from the quay, you will notice the unusual, highly striated cliffs to the right. The travel writer SPB Mais, in his 1938 book Walks in North Devon, describes them as "a glorious assortment of rocks twisted and torn with seams like slices of bacon." They were formed over 300 million years ago by continents crashing together; the huge movements that created them are easy to imagine when you see the dramatically contorted folds of rock in the cliffs.

Hartland Quay itself was built around the end of the 16th century, using the natural rock barrier that connects the shore with Life Rock. The quay curved out into the sea, rather like the one that survives at nearby Clovelly. It was busy for nigh on three centuries, receiving all manner of cargo including coal and limestone from south Wales. At its height it would have been a hive of activity, with goods coming and going, and at one point in the early 19th century it even had its own bank, which issued Hartland Quay notes. However, it fell into decline after the railway came to Bideford in 1855, and a storm in 1887 destroyed it, leaving only a few traces visible at low tide.

Today, the Hartland Quay Hotel is the only commercial concern, but it's a busy one. It's been going since 1886, when the customs house was converted into accommodation. The hotel also runs a museum with displays about the history of the quay and the many ships that have foundered on this stretch of coastline.

The route takes you south along the coast path from Hartland Quay. There are great views of Lundy Island, a distinctive shape on the horizon with its high cliffs. You pass Screda Point, where a sequence of triangular rocks point out to sea, and then you see a pyramid-shaped hill ahead: this is St Catherine's Tor ❷. Just before it you can get down to the oddly named Childspit Beach, which is usually deserted and another lovely place to swim (although the final descent is by a rope which is not for everyone). St Catherine's Tor is so-called because there used to be a medieval chapel at the top, which was possibly part of the monastery at nearby Hartland Abbey; there is no trace of it now.

After passing the tor, a short ascent brings you to the top of the next valley, which is one of many 'hanging valleys' in this part of the world. Characterised by steep sides, these valleys have been cut short and left suspended above the water by the erosion of the cliffs, so their streams do not run

gently down to the shore but end dramatically as waterfalls. The strange thing about this particular valley is that it is home to the biggest waterfall along this stretch of the coast, but as you descend the hill there is no sign of it. It is only when you get to the bottom and can hear the crashing echoes of thousands of tonnes of water falling that you realise it's there. Even then, it's still not visible; you need to walk right to the edge of the cliff to see it, and climb down a short stretch of steep path for the best views.

Speke's Mill Mouth waterfall ❸ really is a magnificent sight. The top section is huge. A curtain of water, about the height of two double decker buses, falls down a black cliff into a pool below. In the winter, when there's been a lot of rain, water covers the entire rock face in what can be a rather terrifying spectacle. The waterfall continues down to the sea with smaller cascades and pools. The top pool is the best to swim in, but we advise going to the beach first, and then rinsing off in the waterfall before continuing on the walk.

After a look at the waterfall, make your way to the beach down a steep path. A lovely pool forms in the rocks near the bottom of this. It's there for around an hour either side of high tide, and the reason for our recommended start time; if you start an hour before high tide, you should find the pool in a good state for swimming. Once the outgoing tide really starts to flow, it soon empties. On a calm day you can still swim out to sea when the pool is emptying, through a gully to the left of the large rock which overlooks the pool. From there, you can have a wonderful exploration around a veritable maze of channels and pools, then head back up to the waterfall for a final dunk before carrying on the walk.

After a play in the waterfall, the walk turns inland, following the stream, which is called Milford Water. The track leads into woods, and then you emerge in the hamlet of Lymebridge ❺. At the crossroads you can do a short diversion (by turning right, over the bridge to find Docton Mill Gardens and Tea Rooms, which have an interesting history. The mill dates back to Saxon times and was still producing flour as late as 1910. Then it became a private house, and in the 1930s it was converted to generate electricity. The current owners, John and Lana Borrett, bought it in 1999, immediately besotted when they saw it advertised in a Sunday newspaper. They did what John described as "the worst property deal I ever conducted in my life", and quit their jobs in London to move down to Devon. Over the years they have created a renowned garden, which you can wander round in the summer months, and afterwards refuel in the tea room.

The next section of the walk takes you uphill along a lane, and then down into another valley,

before emerging in the hamlet of Stoke ❽. The tower of the church is visible from some distance away, and for centuries it was a landmark for mariners out at sea. Dedicated to St Nectan, the church is known as the 'Cathedral of North Devon' and has the unusual distinction of possessing a chair that was used by the Emperor of Ethiopia, Haile Selassie, who visited the village in 1938 after fleeing his country when it was invaded by the Italians. He was offered refuge at nearby Hartland Abbey and, as a Christian, attended church. He even opened the church fête, which made quite a story for the local newspaper.

After a look around the church, you start walking back towards the coast. (To extend the walk, and have another swim, you can turn right at point ❾, just out of Stoke, to head down to Blackpool Mill and Blegberry Beach, then walk south along the coast path back to Hartland Quay.) You will notice a striking ruin on a summit over to the right, close to the cliffs. Marked simply as a tower on the OS map, this is known as the Pleasure House, and was probably a kind of summerhouse for the owners of Hartland Abbey and their guests. The arch is said to have been created to allow a coach and horses to be driven inside to wait while the gentry admired the sea view.

You arrive back in beautiful Hartland Quay. Because of its amazing setting, it has been used in many films, most recently the 2020 Netflix production of Daphne du Maurier's *Rebecca*. The set dressers moved in a month before filming started, working around locals and visitors to create the scene of Rebecca's beach house, with props including lobster pots, horse-drawn carts and an old telephone box. As you leave, look out for the boat which was used in the film, which is now in the upper car park.

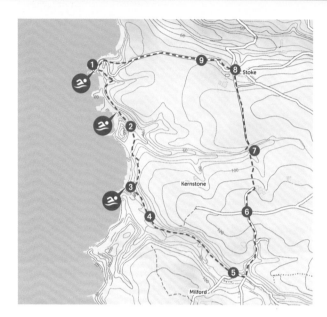

❶ From the lower Hartland Quay Hotel car park you can walk down the quay for a swim before starting the walk. Then take the coast path where it joins the car park at the bottom of the road. Ascend some steep steps and at the top turn right, heading south, hugging the coast with the sea on your right. You will pass a beach where there is a rope to help you get down. This is Childspit beach which is another potential swim spot if you're up for a James Bond style descent.
0.5 miles

❷ Pass St Catherine's Tor, a large conical hill, on your right. Follow the path, keeping as close as you can to the sea on your right. Go over a stile next to a seven-bar metal gate and start to walk uphill, then through a metal gate and descend the hill.
0.4 miles

❸ You arrive at a flat area above the beach at Speke's Mill Mouth. To find the beach, follow the rough path down to your right, near the bottom of the steps. For the waterfall, do not descend to the beach, but go continue ahead to where you can see a rickety fence and hear the sound of the waterfall; there is a gap in the fence where you can climb down to the main fall. After your swim take the track which heads inland, walking with the stream on your right – do not cross the stream.
0.2 miles

❹ You reach a fork. Bear right here, going downhill and into the wooded valley. Pass a single-storey house called Appletrees on your left. Pass a footbridge on your right; do not cross it but keep following the track.
0.6 miles

❺ The track meets a road; turn left. Shortly after, you reach a crossroads with a thatched cottage on the left and a bridge on the right. You can divert right, over the bridge, to visit the Docton Mill garden and Tea Room, but to continue the walk turn left here and begin an ascent up the road. You pass stone gate posts with 'Trellick' on them on your left.
0.5 miles

❻ You reach a crossroads called Kernstone Cross. Carry straight on, signed 'unsuitable for motors'. The track bends to the right, then you reach Wargery Farm and turn left, heading downhill. You will see the church tower ahead of you, and there's also a view of Lundy Island. The track kinks right before heading down into woods.
0.4 miles

❼ You pass through a wooded valley, following the track down and then up again. The track reaches a road at a bend; go straight ahead here, following the road down in the direction of the church tower.
0.5 miles

❽ You arrive in the village at a T-junction with a post box opposite. Turn left and head across to the church. Walk through the churchyard past the church and on the other side take the stone stile on the right with the public footpath sign. Bear right to follow the footpath alongside the road. **0.2 miles**

9 You go through a metal gate and the path forks. Take the left fork, following the wooden public footpath sign. (You can extend the walk by following the right fork down to Blackpool Mill and then heading south along the coast back to Hartland Quay). Keep left to reach another stile beside a seven-bar metal gate; go through and again keep to the left, following the stone wall and hedge. Notice the folly in the distance on your right. Follow the footpath out of the field, between Rocket House on your right and the toll booth on your left, and down the hill to the right of the road, joining it at the last bend to the car park. **0.7 miles**

Walk 3

BLACKCHURCH ROCK
AND CLOVELLY CIRCULAR

A magnificent walk through the picturesque village of Clovelly and a scenic stretch of the North Devon coast, with swims in a harbour and through a natural arch. You can only swim through the arch on a high tide, so start the walk a couple of hours before high water, and bring money to pay for entry to Clovelly village.

INFORMATION

DISTANCE: 6 miles
TIME: Allow 5 hours with stops and swims
MAP OS EXPLORER: 126 Clovelly and Hartland
START POINT & END POINT: Brownsham car park (SS 285 259) EX39 6AN, What3Words: butlers.person.when
PUBLIC TRANSPORT: Bus services 218 or 219 from Bude or 319 from Barnstaple stop at the visitor centre car park; start walking from the coast path above Clovelly.
SWIMMING: Clovelly Harbour (SS 31864 24857) and Mouthmill Beach (SS 29814 26556). These are best swum in the top half of the tide; it is only possible to swim under Blackchurch Rock at Mouthmill Beach at high tide.
REFRESHMENTS: The New Inn, halfway down the village is a great historic pub and a perfect stop for refreshments (01237 431303, EX39 5TQ). The Red Lion Hotel on the quayside has top-notch eating in the Harbour Restaurant or more chilled vibes in The Snug and Harbour Bar; accommodation is also available (01237 431237 EX39 5TF)
EASIER ACCESS: The Visitor Centre Reception above the village can book you a seat in a Land Rover to take you down to the harbour and back up, for which there is a small charge. You can enter the water from the harbour steps on a high tide. Unfortunately, Mouthmill Beach is not accessible at all.
NEARBY SWIM SPOTS: Peppercombe, a little further east, is a beautifully remote beach which feels really wild. You can walk there through the woods from Bucks Mills.

Today's walk starts at the Brownsham National Trust car park ❶ and quickly takes us down wooded tracks and along bridleways into some beautiful countryside. Brownsham Wood is a great place to test your tree knowledge, as you might be able to spot birch, hazel, ash and oak here, before the paths take you up into rolling fields ❷ and pasturelands. Indeed, you will pass an impressive oak as you arrive at Court Farm ❸ and walk past a thatched summerhouse with a plaque bearing the initials CH.

We are now in the heart of the Clovelly estate, which was originally the property of William the Conqueror, the king of England. Unusually, even the village is entirely privately owned, and has been associated with only three families since the mid-13th century, including the Hamlyn family who acquired it in 1738. Christine Hamlyn – she of the initials CH - inherited the estate in 1884, and along with her husband renovated many village cottages, hence the initials you will see on several properties along the route, including the summerhouse. John Rous, the current owner, is her great grand-nephew.

The walk heads onto a lane up to All Saints, the medieval parish church of Clovelly ❹, which is west of the manor house at Clovelly Court. The church can be visited and contains several mural monuments and monumental brasses to the Cary family, who were lords of the manor before the Hamlyns.

The route continues through Clovelly Court Gardens (£5), open 10am–4pm every day, or past them and then turning left into the lane down to the village. The gardens are home to greenhouses with fruits like peaches, figs and lemons, as well as vegetables, herbaceous plants and vines. All benefit from being situated in this sheltered, sunny corner of North Devon, where the warmth of the North Atlantic Current encourages the plants to thrive. Much of the produce is used to supply the Red Lion Hotel (which we will pass later), with some also available to buy.

The walk now takes us into the village of Clovelly itself ❺, where there is an entry fee (£8.75) towards the upkeep of this fascinating time capsule. The steep, cobbled main thoroughfare drops 122 metres to the harbour in just half a mile, and the walk takes us through some of the historic cottages before arriving at this pedestrianised street with its residential dwellings, craft shops, galleries, chapels, the Kingsley Museum and the New Inn. Clovellians (the name for the locals, and not some alien foe from Doctor Who) call the main cobbled

street 'Up-Along' or 'Down-Along' depending on whether they are ascending or descending the vertiginous hill.

Charles Dickens renamed the village Steepways in his 1892 short story *A Message from the Sea* and described it as "built sheer up the face of a steep and lofty cliff. There was no road in it, there was no wheeled vehicle in it, there was not a level yard in it. From the sea-beach to the cliff-top two irregular rows of white houses, placed opposite to one another, and twisting here and there, and there and here, rose, like the sides of a long succession of stages of crooked ladders, and you climbed up the village or climbed down the village by the staves between, some six feet wide or so, and made of sharp irregular stones… No two houses in the village were alike, in chimney, size, shape, door, window, gable, roof-tree, anything."

It would be possible to write a whole book about this village, which is often described as the prettiest in Devon. John Rous rents out all the homes in the village to local people; there are no holiday homes, and living here comes with its own challenges, as cars are banned. In the past, donkeys carried everything from beer barrels to laundry bags and rubbish; today, everything is carried up and down by the sleds you will spot as you walk the cobbles. One local told us about a piano being brought down by sled and the owner pausing for a rest and to play a tune or two.

The village also has some intriguing traditions. On Shrove Tuesday, they host Lentsherd, which sees children meeting at dusk to chase away bad spirits and drive the devil into the sea, armed with tin cans on string. They set off Down-Along, making as much clattering noise as possible, before tying all the cans together and throwing them into the harbour (and retrieving them again).

The Clovelly Herring Festival takes place every November to celebrate the return of the 'silver darlins' on their annual migration. The village once depended on the harvest of herring, but today there are just two fishermen, who employ sustainable methods using small-scale nets and long lines.

The picturesque village has inspired everyone artists like Rex Whistler and JMW Turner and writers including Charles Dickens, Rudyard Kipling and Charles Kingsley. The latter grew up in the village, where his father was the rector. His novel, *Westward Ho!* helped boost tourism in what was at the time a little-known area of North Devon. The Charles Kingsley Museum is in the cottage where the author lived as a child, where you will also find a mural of his other famous book, *The Water Babies*.

The walk continues down to the harbour ❻, which makes a great spot for a swim; the best time is the top half of the tide. The quay is as historic as it looks, built in the 13th century and extended in Tudor Times, when seafarers like Sir Francis Drake, Sir Walter Raleigh and Sir Richard Grenville were frequent visitors. Look out for the four bollards in the quay, which are said to be cannon barrels from the Spanish Armada.

One of the beautiful old cottages overlooking the harbour is called Crazy Kate's Cottage. It once belonged to Kate Lyall, who would watch her husband from the upstairs window as he fished in the bay. One day a squall blew up and she looked on helplessly as the waves swept him to his death. She became demented with grief until one day in 1736 she put on her wedding dress and walked out into the sea to join her husband in his watery grave.

The lifeboat station was built in 1870 following a huge storm that sank most of the fishing boats, costing the lives of many local fishermen. When the RNLI boat was taken out of service in 1988, the villagers set up their own inshore rescue boat until the RNLI returned eight years later. In 2000 the station was extended and modernised, and it is open to the public in the summer months.

We had great fun swimming here in the summer, as well as jumping in from the harbour wall – the tide needs to be high enough to cover the steps up to the wall before you attempt this. It's also lovely to stroll along the beach. Walk out past the lifeboat station and look for the waterfall; there's a cave behind, where King Arthur's magician, Merlin is said to have been born. Off the coast you will be able to spot Lundy, and a small ferry operates to the island from the quay in the summer months.

As you'd imagine, this picturesque village and harbour has been a location for several films and television series including a star-studded production of *Treasure Island* (1990), the Oscar-winning *Sense and Sensibility* (2008) and the charmingly atmospheric *Guernsey Literary and Potato Peel Pie Society* (2018). It was also the setting for several episodes of *Jeeves and Wooster* starring Hugh

Laurie and Stephen Fry, and even one of the Foster's lager ads starring Paul Hogan of *Crocodile Dundee* fame.

The walk continues through the tunnel under the Red Lion, which dates back to the 18th century and was originally a line of fisherman's cottages. The Snug bar is a cosy spot to enjoy a pint of Clovelly Cobbler beer or perhaps a local cider. It's a great place to meet the locals and find out what life in the village is like, or perhaps chat to a fisherman about the 'one that got away.'

Don't over-indulge though, as there is a steep climb up the lane to join the coast path ❼. This takes you through parkland and across meadows, before entering into woodland. Along the route, you can enjoy views up to Clovelly Court, which has been the family seat of the Hamlyns and their descendants since it was built in 1740. The walk passes an ornate shelter called Angel's Wings ❽ built in 1826, one of several shelters commissioned around the estate by Sir James Hamlyn Williams. His daughter, Lady Chichester, lived across the bay and he would apparently sit here looking over to where she lived. The elaborate carvings were made by a former butler at Clovelly Court.

Next we head up onto a heathland known as Gallantry Bower ❾, 100 metres above the shoreline. On the clifftop, you can make out the remains of a bowl barrow or tumulus. This Bronze Age burial mound is possibly linked to the ancient hillfort at Windbury Head to the west. As we continue there are some great views down to the sea below and you might be able to spot the fulmars who make the towering cliffs their home. Look out for Blackchurch Rock, which is the next potential swim spot, once we drop down at Mouth Mill ❿.

The beach is pretty pebbly, with a stream running out to sea that would once have helped power the mill that gives the beach its name. To the right you will be able to see the imposing triangular formation of Blackchurch Rock. On a low tide you can walk around it and through the two 'windows', while on a high tide and with calm seas, you can swim right through it. The shale and sandstone stack has been separated from the nearby cliffs by sea erosion, while wave action carved out the mudstone to create the arches in the stack.

It's a real adventure to swim through the arch at high water, but it goes without saying that you should only attempt this when the conditions are completely calm. When we visited, we lucked out on the weather conditions which were perfect. Any nerves we may have had soon vanished when we met John Rous, (the owner of Clovelly) who plunged into the sea and swam through the arches, before diving from the rock itself. It's a really magical spot for a swim and explore and on a warm summer's day, and hard to imagine that the remote cove was once a hive of nefarious smuggling activity. It was also the site of more honest activities: as you continue the walk you will pass an old lime kiln. Here limestone was heated with coal transported across from south Wales to make quicklime, used to fertilise the nearby fields.

The walk zig-zags up through woods and fields ⓫ taking you back to the car park where we started. And what memories you will have, of a walk that has taken in kings and pirates, cannibals and tragic brides, and some of the most beautiful coastline in the country. As Captain Jorgan, one of Charles Dicken's characters described it, "a mighty sing'lar and pretty place it is, as ever I saw in all the days of my life."

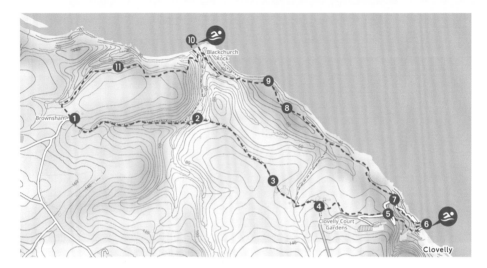

1 From the entrance to the car park go down the steps onto a lane, and bear left down to some farm buildings; turn right following sign for Mouthmill. Follow the track downhill through woods with a stream on your right. Cross the stream and turn left at the T-junction.
0.9 miles

2 You reach a fork. Turn right uphill, following the bridleway sign. The track bears right and you reach a seven-bar metal gate with 'bull in field' warning sign. Go through the gate and walk up the left-hand side of the field past a deer observation tower on your left. Continue into next field and head diagonally right towards gate in the distance. Exit through a wooden gate and walk along the track following blue public footpath sign.
0.6 miles

3 Walk through farm buildings and then past a thatched summer house on right. Follow the lane over a bridge and then uphill. (It is possible to turn left just after the bridge to reach the coast path avoiding Clovelly and rejoin the route to Blackchurch Rock.)
0.4 miles

4 You reach a junction with a church ahead. Bear right following green signs for the gardens. You arrive at Clovelly Court Gardens and a stone arched doorway. Our route now goes through Clovelly Court Gardens (£5); if they are closed, walk on to the gates ahead and turn left for Clovelly. Walk past the glasshouses on your left towards the rear wall, then turn left and immediately right into the main gardens. Follow the left-hand side towards a tennis court ahead. Turn left before the courts and

through the blue metal gate, then turn right and walk through the trees, following the path downhill.
0.5 miles

5 You reach a large black metal and wood gate with green fence posts. Go through and cross the lane, walking past a wooden shed into a small parking area. Turn left down steps by stone wall and follow the steep path down into the village, turning left at the end down the main cobbled street.
0.3 miles

6 At the harbour, stop for a swim before walking through tunnel under the Red Lion and up the very steep lane.
0.2 miles

7 As the lane bends sharply to the left, you will see a five-bar black gate with green posts on

your right. Turn right off the lane through the gate and follow the path (there is no public footpath sign, but this is correct). You are now on the coast path, which you follow with the sea on your right.
0.3 miles

8 Arrive at the distinctive carved Angel Wings seat. Continue following the coast path.
0.9 miles

9 Pass across Gallantry Bower before following the coast path downhill.
0.2 miles

10 At the bottom off the hill is a flat area with old buildings. Make

your way down onto beach to the right for a swim. After, walk up to the buildings, and then turn right following the acorn finger post. Zig-zag up through woods and emerge into a meadow following National Trust sign for Brownsham. Follow the path through two fields with the sea on your right.
0.7 miles

11 Go through a small wooden gate and turn left (to visit Winbury Head carry straight on). Stay on path through fields and woods, following signs for Brownsham, past a footbridge on your right, until the path forks left to take you back to the car park.
0.5 miles

WESTWARD HO! AND APPLEDORE

This wonderful walk takes you from the bustling seaside town of Westward Ho! to the pretty fishing village of Appledore via a spectacular country park. There are swims in tidal pools, the open sea, and from a lifeboat slipway. We have included two optional 'spurs' to two extra swim locations.

INFORMATION

DISTANCE: 7 miles, 8.5 miles with a visit to Mermaid's Pool
TIME: Allow all day
MAP: OS Explorer 139 Bideford, Ilfracombe & Barnstaple.
START AND END POINT: Main Car Park on Golf Links Road (SS 432 292, EX39 1LH, What3Words park. mirror.scouts)
PUBLIC TRANSPORT: the route 21 bus runs from Barnstaple, which is the nearest mainline station
SWIMMING: the Rock Pool for two hours either side of low tide (SS 428 292), Mermaid's Pool for one hour either side of low tide (SS 418 289), RNLI Station at Sandymere, best in the top half of the tide (SS 437 304), Appledore lifeboat slipway for an hour either side of high tide (SS 459 309), and Appledore quay steps at all states of the tide (SS 465 306)
REFRESHMENTS: Pebble Ridge Kitchen at the Northam Burrows Visitor Centre (01237 424138, EX39 1XS). The Coffee Cabin at Appledore is a friendly wild swimmer hangout in a stunning quayside location (01237 475843, EX39 1QS).
EASIER ACCESS: You can park fairly close to the RNLI Station at Sandymere Beach, although you will still need to cross the pebbles. There are various slipways and steps into the water at Appledore, including the lifeboat slipway and the quay steps
NEARBY SWIM SPOTS: Saunton Sands boasts three-and-a-half miles of golden sands, backed by impressive dunes. Bucks Mills, midway between Westward Ho! and Clovelly, is a pretty secluded cove with a waterfall and some sand to swim from at a low tide

oday's walk takes a little bit of planning, because the various swims along it require different states of the tide. At the start, in Westward Ho!, there are two tidal pools which are only accessible around low water; while in Appledore, several miles into the route, high tide is best. Set off from Westward Ho! around low tide to give yourself the most swimming options (see directions for more details), and pace the walk with swims and stops, so as to arrive at Appledore as high tide approaches.

Westward Ho! ❶, is a busy seaside village known for being the only place in the British Isles to have an exclamation mark in its name. The resort was named by Victorian entrepreneurs eager to capitalise on the success of Charles Kingsley's novel *Westward Ho!*, which was set in nearby Bideford. Seaside tourism and sea bathing were growing in popularity, and the developers initially opened a hotel in the 1860s and called it (we kid you not) the Westward Ho!-tel. Then the adjacent villas were named after the book, and then eventually the whole resort. Trivia fans may like to know that the only other place in the world with an exclamation mark in its name is the Canadian municipality of Saint-Louis-du-Ha!-Ha!, which had to go one better by having two of them.

A famous past resident of Westward Ho! was Rudyard Kipling, who spent several of his childhood years in the resort. As you walk along the promenade towards the brightly coloured beach huts, you can see the first stanza of his poem *If—* set into the pavement on the promenade in granite setts. It was voted the nation's favourite poem in a BBC poll. And 'if' you fancy going for a swim in a tidal pool, while others are walking right by, then the man-made Rock Pool ❷ is waiting for you. Built from a natural rock pool and dating back at least 120 years, it was closed due to storm damage in 2014, but was refurbished the following year thanks to a Coastal Community Grant.

The pool is fairly shallow (around 1.2 metres at the deep end) but still great for a refreshing dip. It's exposed about two hours either side of low water, and it's worth wearing swim shoes to protect you from the limpets and barnacles. It is a really special place for a swim, amid the surrounding moonscape of rocks and with the expanse of the Atlantic out in front of you. In 2023, the pool had to be closed temporarily and drained when thousands of whitebait and sand eels became stranded in it. More famously, a basking shark washed up on the beach in 2003 and was later sold at auction for $17 million dollars. However, that was after it had been preserved in formaldehyde and named *Leviathan* by Damien Hirst.

There is also another tidal pool further west, which is known as the Mermaid's Pool ❷ᴬ (main picture), which is worth a visit if you have time. However, it is only accessible one hour either side of low tide so you will need to adjust your timings if you want to visit it. (We have included this as an optional spur but if you wish to do this you will need to set off about an hour before low water). It is about 0.7 miles from the Rock Pool, or half an hour's walk. You get to it by walking along the old sewer pipe west to its end and then picking your way over the rocks to the south-west. As the name suggests, it's a magical place to take a dip, and don't forget your goggles as you will be swimming in what is in effect a giant rock pool. There are often

fish swimming with you, although we didn't spot any mermaids while we were there.

The walk returns to the touristy main resort and past takeaways and ice cream shops towards the famous pebble ridge ❸, which was created by collapses along the sandstone cliffs found between Westward Ho! and Hartland Point. The action of the waves polished the rocks to create smooth grey pebbles, while a process called longshore drift has transported them to create the ridge that protects Westward Ho! Beach from the Atlantic. You can climb up onto the ridge to enjoy fine views, but don't try walking along it for any distance as it's extremely tough going and could lead to a twisted ankle. The ridge also provides a defensive arm for Northam Burrows Country Park, which we will be walking through. This is a 253-hectare SSSI and an integral part of North Devon's UNESCO Biosphere Reserve.

The Burrows is a lovely grassy coastal plain of salt marsh, sand dunes and grasslands, and is easy walking. All sorts of rare plants flourish here, including the pyramid orchid, strawberry clove, scarlet pimpernel, henbane and evening primrose. Also look out for the sharp rush, with sharp-tipped stems that people say can pierce a golf ball; its presence here is quite apt, as the Burrows is also home to Royal North Devon Golf Club, which was founded in 1864 and is the oldest golf course in England. Golfers share the park with ponies, sheep and walkers, and the club was the first to ban plastic tees over fears they were being eaten by wildlife.

The walk passes a concrete slat path over the ridge down to the beach ❹ known by locals as 'sponge fingers' because that's exactly what it looks like. It's possible to swim here, next to the RNLI station (open mid-May to mid-September) and off a Blue Flag beach. After a dip and back on the route, you will pass a small body of water known as Sandymere, which looks very tempting for a swim but is actually very shallow. Just beyond the lake is the Northam Burrows Visitor Centre ❺, with toilets, a café called the Pebble Ridge Kitchen and an exhibition centre housing a mini aquarium and displays about local wildlife and the threats to the local landscape presented by sea level rise and climate change. The walk then continues around the headland with great views of Baggy Point to the north, and then bends around to the right, following the estuary on the left. The beach here is not safe for swimming, due to strong currents.

Walking alongside the estuary, you can see the lifeboat slipway up ahead at Appledore; this is the next swim spot. There's a bit more walking to do first, as the route bears around to the right ❻ passing a salt marsh called The Skern which is known for its biodiversity. It is visited by several species of birds including waders like curlews, oystercatchers and little egrets. In the winter, Brent geese fly back here from the Arctic to escape the harsh conditions. Gulls and terns are also a common sight.

The walk now leaves the Burrows past the toll booth ❼ and heads down towards Appledore, along either the shore on a low tide or a road and path at high tide. The next swim spot is at the lifeboat slipway at what is known as Bad Step ❽. It is best at high water, and hopefully, your timings will have worked and you will be arriving there at the optimum time. It is a popular spot for local swimmers, with fantastic views up the estuary and out to the open sea.

If it's too rough for swimming, which was the case last time we visited, it is usually calm further round at the quay steps ❽ᴬ; this is the second optional spur of the walk. The steps are about half a mile away and easy to find: just keep walking along the shore until you reach them. There are several sets of steps into the water, and it's fun to swim down and then get out at the next set of steps and walk back to the start. Appledore itself is a very pretty fishing village with colourful houses and winding streets to explore. It's also home to a fantastic book festival every September that celebrates 'Literature & The Arts by the Sea'.

The walk returns along the inland side of The Burrows ❾ and ❿, where it is very likely you will see ponies and sheep. The area is common land dating back to when it was part of the ancient manor of Northam. Apparently, the rights allow 1,200 sheep and 100 horses to graze there, although we gave up counting. You may also spot some old concrete bases, which are the remains of a Second World War radar station. You will cross attractive bridges over the Pill, a tidal stream that flows from Goosypool (at the south end of The Burrows) to the Skern saltmarsh. On a spring tide, sea water flows up the Pill in the opposite direction from Appledore Bridge, and after big storms it can takes days for the water to drain away again. The walk returns into Westward Ho!, where we think you should treat yourself to an ice-cream.

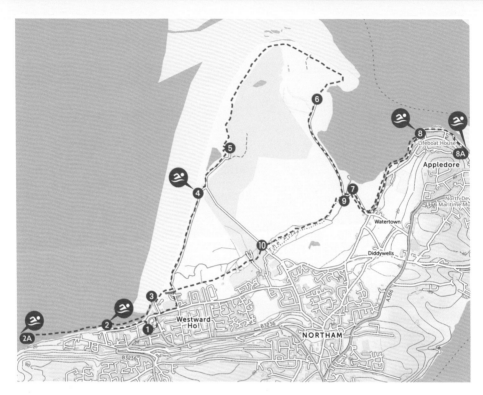

Start the walk at low tide to include the Mermaid's Pool, or 1-2 hours after low tide for just the Rock Pool; leave Westward Ho! three hours before high tide if wishing to swim at the lifeboat slip at Appledore.

1 From the car park, head to the seafront and turn left. Walk along the promenade with the sea on your right, past the huge blue block of flats and then some beach huts. Look to your right to see the Rock Pool, and walk down the steps to get to it.
0.3 miles

2 From the pool, you can walk west along the pipeline to find the natural Mermaid Pool **2A**, for an hour either side of low tide. This will add about 1.4 miles to the walk and take you about half an hour each way. That's quite a bit on an already long walk, so this is an optional extra. After, return to the sea pool and walk east along the promenade with the sea on your left, passing the blue flats and the building with a roof like sails.
1 mile from Mermaid Pool, 0.3 miles from Rock Pool

3 You reach a slipway down to the beach and continue walking past takeaways and shops. Pass the small car park on your right and go through a wooden gate by the start of the pebble ridge. Turn right along a boardwalk and then left along the road past the shed where people pay to park. Walk with the pebble ridge on your left. You might be tempted to walk along the top of it so you can see the sea but that is very hard going!
0.8 miles

4 You reach a lifeguards' hut with a distinctive concrete path (known as 'sponge fingers' by locals); you could stop for a swim here. Otherwise carry on along the shore, passing a shallow body of water called Sandymere, and head towards the information centre.
0.3 miles

5 At the information centre, you can stop for some refreshment and find out more about Northam Burrows. After, carry on walking through the dunes with the sea on your left. Pass the golf course on the right, and follow the path as it bears right around the headland and along the estuary.
1.5 miles

6 Join the road and pass a shallow area of water on your right. Cross a stone bridge and follow the road as it bears left.
0.7 miles

7 You reach the hut where people pay to enter the Burrows. From here there are two options. At low tide, you can follow the

sign left and walk along the shore to the lifeboat station; at high, follow the road for a short distance and then turn left at the cross roads. Walk along the road until you reach the Watertown Garage. Here you can bear left off the road following the coast path sign, and walk the path all the way to the Appledore lifeboat slipway.
0.8 miles high-tide route,
0.5 miles low-tide route

8 At the slipway, have a swim. If conditions are rough here, you may still find you can swim at the quayside **8A** where there are numerous sets of steps down into the water. For the quayside, carry on walking from the slipway with the sea on your left. Pass the Beaver Inn, go through a car park by the sea wall, and you will reach the quayside. It's about half a mile from the lifeboat slipway so this will add about a mile onto the walk. After your swim, retrace your steps back into Northam Burrows, passing the toll hut again.
0.8 miles high-tide route,
0.5 miles low-tide route

9 At the stone bridge, turn left, following the red trail line and arrow on posts. You're now walking along the southern boundary of Northam Burrows. Cross a small humpback bridge. Pass some red brick lodge-like buildings on your left and bear right.
0.6 miles

10 Cross the road and then and a small boardwalk with an information sign beside it.; you are now following the blue trail. Pass a long white fence on your left with a pitch and putt behind it. Keep following the trail with various boardwalks to arrive back at the parking payment shed you passed at the beginning. Turn left here and pass the cricket ground on your right. At the crossroads at the end of the ground turn right into Golf Links Road. Pass some brightly coloured houses on your right and then turn left along a path to the left of the Waterfront pub. At the end bear right back into the car park.
1 mile

Walk 5

VELATOR QUAY AND CROW POINT

A fascinating walk through an ever-changing landscape, taking in a dune headland that feels like a desert island and farmland being reclaimed by the waves, with swims in the sea and a tidal river. You need to start the walk two to three hours before high water.

INFORMATION

TIME: 4 hours
DISTANCE: 6 miles
MAP: OS Explorer 139 Bideford, Ilfracombe & Barnstaple
START AND END POINT: car park at Velator Quay (SS 484 354, EX33 2DX, What3Words: eyeful.creeps.fulfilled)
PUBLIC TRANSPORT: the 303 bus between Barnstaple and Woolacombe stops in Braunton, as do the 21, 21A and 21C buses from Barnstaple and Bideford
SWIMMING: Velator Quay only at high tide (SS 484 353), the lagoon behind Crow Point (best at top half of tide) (SS 465 322), so start your walk 2–3 hours before high tide
REFRESHMENTS: None on the walk. The Quay Café is very near the start of the walk and serves pizzas as well as snacks and sandwiches (01271 268180, EX33 2DX). The dog-friendly Wild Thyme Café in nearby Braunton serves smoothies and juices, wraps and baguettes (01271 815191, EX33 1EE)
EASIER ACCESS: there's a slipway next to the wooden jetty at Velator Quay, so you can easily walk into the water. You can also pay a toll shortly after Velator Quay to drive down to the car park at Crow Point, which is right next to the water
NEARBY SWIM SPOTS: Saunton Sands is famous for its surf but also has a community of people who swim there regularly

The magical thing about today's walk is that you are always aware of the moving tide; the surroundings on the route are constantly changing with the ebb and flow of the sea. There are two swims: at the start-and-end point of Velator Quay ❶, where you can only swim for an hour either side of high water, and halfway around the walk at Crow Point ❺, which is best swum in the top half of the tide. For optimum swimming, start the walk two to three hours before high water, so that you can walk out to the farthest point and have a swim there, then swim again at the end.

Velator Quay on the River Caen is now a quiet backwater where people keep leisure boats and folk come to walk and enjoy the peace. However, in the past it was a hive of activity, a busy port that helped nearby Braunton grow from a small agricultural village to a prosperous trading centre. The river here, whose old name is Braunton Pill, is completely tidal, draining out at low tide into the Taw/Torridge estuary; boats moored here can only be accessed at high water.

The landscape as we see it today – including the river – is the result of a huge programme of human intervention in the 19th century. Until this time the whole area was salt marsh, where people harvested seaweed and cockles. However local entrepreneurs saw an opportunity to make money by reclaiming the land for pasture and therefore increasing its value.

Work started in 1811 on a complex system of ditches and sluices to hold back the sea, culminating by 1815 in the creation of a

large embankment to protect the whole area. This became known as the Great Sea Wall and allowed a large area of land to be reclaimed. A few decades later, work started on straightening the river as well, so that larger vessels could get in to Braunton. In 1870, a quay was built at Velator for exporting farm produce and importing goods such as coal, bricks and limestone. An interesting information board at the quay shows an old black and white photo of some of the boats that used to dock here, including river barges, wooden ketches and square topsail schooners.

From Velator, the route heads south-west alongside the river, where you soon find yourself walking on the top of a large bank. This is actually the Great Sea Wall, and it is quite remarkable to think it has held back the sea for over two centuries. You'll cross over several unusual stone and slate stiles, which are part of walls created to mark the field boundaries when the land was reclaimed.

Once you reach the end of the river, you will see a flooded area to your left with some ruined buildings; this is Horsey Island, which isn't actually an island, but another area that was reclaimed in the 19th century. It was protected by a second embankment further out, built in the 1850s, but this was breached by a storm in 2017, and the area is now returning to its original state as an intertidal wetland habitat. The coast path used to run alongside the outer wall, so you could walk on either side of the 'island', but that has now been closed. Devon Wildlife Trust took over the area in 2019 and considered repairing the bank and restoring the footpath, but the costs were prohibitive, with no guarantee that the defence would not be breached again. The developing habitat of mudflats, sandbanks and saltmarsh is proving very attractive to many birds, including, egrets, spoonbills and ospreys, but the lack of protection from the sea is very worrying for some local people.

After about 2 miles the walk arrives at the White House ❷, a solitary building right by the beach, marked as 'Crow Beach House' on the OS map. It used to be known as the Ferry House, because up until Victorian times there was a ferry service between here and Appledore on the other side of the estuary. The house stands in isolation here and in 2018, after the breach of the embankment, the plight of its anxious owner made local and national news stories, expressing great concern at the vulnerability of her property. Despite a public campaign calling for action to protect the area, it seems highly unlikely that any public bodies will spend funds on more sea defences, so the house does indeed look vulnerable.

After the White House, the route continues through a car park and then crosses a narrow road ❸. Built in 1943, this is known locally as the American Road; this area was the Assault Training Centre, where American GIs practised raiding pillboxes and other obstacles ahead of the D-Day landings. You're now walking through the Braunton Burrows dunes, named for the rabbits that were introduced into the area in Norman times. It's one of the largest sand dune systems in the British Isles, at about 1,000 square hectares. It is also an SSSI, home to nearly 500 species of flowering plants including 11 orchids, 33 species of butterfly, and five of our six native reptiles. In the summer you will see lots of flowers include large blue viper's bugloss and bright yellow St John's wort.

The route passes through what are called the 'slacks': these are dips and flat areas in the lower part of the dune landscape. You walk along a patchy boardwalk, made of sleepers from the nearby Tarka railway line that was grubbed up during the Beeching cuts of the late 1960s.

After walking up and down over the dunes for a short time, you reach the sea at an area called The Neck. ❹. Walking out from the dunes into this vast expanse of sand and water, with driftwood everywhere and fading wooden groynes, feels very special. There are stunning views as far as the eye can see, and it feels as though you've landed on a desert island. Although it's tempting to get in the water here, there are strong currents in the estuary, so swimming is not advised. It is safer to keep walking and swim a little further on, behind Crow Point.

The route takes you back towards up the estuary. As you walk along the beach with the sea on your right, you will notice a large rock barrier on your left; another effort to keep back the sea. At the end of the barrier is what looks like a small dune island. This is Crow Point, which in the past was much busier. A lighthouse was built here in the early 19th century, there was also a ferry service, and it's thought there was a chapel here too, although no trace of it now remains. The only modern feature is an automated warning light, which is further south than the original.

Bear left behind Crow Point, and you will find the swim spot ❺. This is a lagoon-like area which fills up at high tide, and where a few boats are moored. It's the perfect place to swim, protected from the currents out in the estuary, and you can enjoy a languid dip in what feels like something of a watery haven.

After, continue walking and you will soon find yourself back at the White House ❷, from where you can retrace your steps to the start. By now, the tide will be fully in, and you can enjoy a final swim from the attractive wooden jetty at Velator Quay. If you don't fancy getting in off the jetty there is a slipway just next to it, or you can just wade in from the bank behind the jetty. When we last visited, the water felt wonderfully clean and fresh, and it was great to wash off the salt from the previous swim. After your dip, it's a short hop back to the car park.

1 From the car park, turn left, cross over the Boundary Drain onto the path, and start to walk along the path with the river on your left. Cross over several unusual stone stiles. Keep following the river, walking with the road on your right. Eventually the path makes a pronounced turn to the right.
1.9 miles

2 You reach a gate and a stile with a house visible behind. Go through the gate: you are by the White House/Crow Beach House on your left, with an entrance to the beach ahead. Do not go onto the beach; bear right along a rough road and walk through the car park. At the end take the small path by the fence where there is an information board with a wooden otter on top.
0.4 miles

3 You reach a sandy road; cross it and take the small path to the left of a green sign saying Christie Estates, Braunton Burrows Conservation area. Follow the sandy path (which at times has the remains of a boardwalk on it) up and down through the dunes until you reach the beach.
0.4 miles

4 At the beach, turn left and walk along the shore with the sea on your right. You will pass a large rock barrier on your left and see the lighthouse at Crow Point ahead. Before reaching the lighthouse, and just before a prominent 'island' of dune, cross left over the rock barrier towards a lagoon with boats.
0.6 miles

5 At the lagoon, behind Crow Point, you can have a swim. Afterwards, retrace your steps for a short distance, and then bear right following the edge of the lagoon. Continue walking with the sea on your right until you get back to the car park and Crow Beach House. From here, retrace your steps. Just before you reach the car park you can have a swim off the jetty at Velator Quay; after, continue back to the car park.
2.7 miles

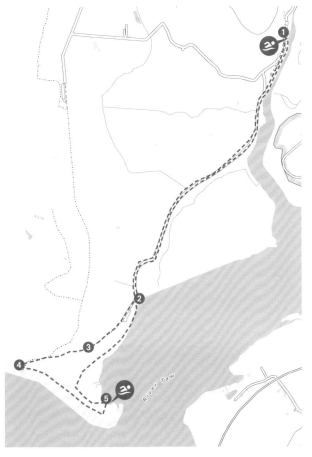

Walk 6

BAGGY POINT, THE MERMAID POOL AND CAVES

A bracing stomp around a magnificent headland with swims in pools, caves and a tunnel, as well as in the famous surf at Croyde. Start the walk around three hours before high tide; to explore the caves you need calm conditions, and to be a competent open water swimmer.

Baggy Point sits between the golden sands of Croyde and Putsborough, with fantastic views across Bideford Bay to Clovelly, Hartland and Lundy. It is a truly beautiful coastal environment, with gorse, heather and wild flowers in abundance. The whole area is owned by the National Trust, who were given the land in 1939 by Edwin, Connie and Florence Hyde, three siblings who had lived there since the late 19th century, after making money in the newspaper industry.

The walk starts from the National Trust car park at the northern end of Croyde Bay ❶, and heads west following the coast path. You'll soon pass some strange preserved bones by the side of the path; they are all that remains of a large whale that was washed up on Croyde Beach in 1915. You will then notice a distinctive modern building to the right; this is Baggy House, which was built in 1994, on the site of a Victorian mansion which was the home of the Hyde family. It is a stark white structure, full of dramatic angles and enormous windows, including one sea-facing glass wall that disappears into the floor.

A short while after passing Baggy House you reach Baggy Point pond, another reminder of the Hyde family's influence on the area. They built it as part of an extension to their garden and kept ducks here. It's not a tempting swimming prospect though, being covered in green weed! The route continues west along the coast path, where you'll soon find a set of old steps leading down to what we call the Mermaid Pool ❷.

INFORMATION

TIME: 4 hours
DISTANCE: 4 miles
MAP: OS Explorer Map 139 Bideford, Ilfracombe and Barnstaple
START AND END POINT: National Trust car park at Baggy Point (SS 432 397, EX33 1FF, What3Words: trunk. reacting.multiples)
PUBLIC TRANSPORT: the 21C bus between Ilfracombe and Barnstaple stops in Croyde
SWIMMING: the beach at Croyde (SS 433 394), Mermaid Pool on the south side of Baggy Point (SS 425 401), swim-through tunnel on south side of Baggy Point (SS 423 402). The swims are best done in the top half of the tide, so start the walk 3 hours before high tide
REFRESHMENTS: The Sandleigh Tea Room by the car park at Baggy Point has a beautiful garden (EX22 1PA, 01271 890930). The Café Croyde Bay has a fantastic location overlooking the sea (EX33 1PA, 01272 891200)
EASIER ACCESS: There's a slipway at the northern side of Croyde beach but you would need to swim at high water to avoid having to climb over rocks; direct access to the sand is from Beach Road, and a car park accessed through the Croyde Burrows campground. The Mermaid Pool is a short walk along the coast path from the car park, with about 20 steps down to the rocks
NEARBY SWIM SPOTS: Barricane Beach at Woolacombe is lovely, particularly at high tide when it fills up like a swimming pool; Putsborough is also good at high water

You'll see the remains of an old concrete platform and a wall on the rocks; this is the site of another of the Hyde family's projects. They built a small harbour here where they could haul their boats up out of the water. Not much of it remains, but the steps and the concrete provide great access to a beautiful lagoon and numerous rocky channels. This is a fabulous place to swim, looking back at the crowds at Croyde beach who appear like ants in the distance. It is accessible on all states of the tide, but is best in the top half; needless to say, you should only swim in calm conditions. On a warm, still day it is like being in the Mediterranean as you pootle around the maze of gullies. Do take goggles, as there are seaweeds, sponges and fish to see if the water is clear.

If the sea is flat calm, and as long as you are a competent open water swimmer, you can head out of the pool to the right, and swim west along the coast for a short distance (about 350 metres) to find caves and a tunnel ❸ you can swim through. At low tide the tunnel dries out; the best time to try it is between mid and high tide. (Hence the recommendation to start the walk about 3 hours before high water). Do use a tow float if you swim this route.

You can also access the caves and tunnel from the shore, by heading back to the coast path, walking west, and then getting down onto the rocks. However, this involves a lot of scrambling and climbing (these cliffs are popular with climbers) so you should only attempt it if you are physically strong and confident. Ideally, it's best to swim there from the Mermaid Pool.

If you do want to climb down, the spot is to be found about ❺ minutes' walk further west from the Mermaid Pool. You will see a concrete box with a metal top by the side of the path (❸), with a faint path off to the left. Go down the path and

scramble down the rocks where you will arrive at a flat area. From here, you can climb down a concrete-covered pipe to the rocks below.

Once at the end of the pipe, you can descend the rocks into the water on the left-hand side (facing Croyde). From here, if you swim to the left, you will find the tunnel that fills up at high tide, which you can swim through (it runs beneath the bit of cliff you've just climbed down), and also caves. Obviously, conditions are hugely variable, according to the size of the tide and the weather conditions. This swim should only be done when there is no wind and the sea is completely calm. If you swim it at high water, you need to be aware of the risk of banging your head on the ceiling of the tunnel. Warnings aside, if you swim here in the right conditions, it is a wonderful adventure – but please exercise caution.

The walk continues along the coast path, rounding the headland at the most westerly extreme of Baggy Point. You'll see an enormous flat slab of sandstone, which is very popular with climbers, and then, after ascending some steps, you'll pass a small sign explaining this area's role in D Day.

In 1944 the Allies were preparing for what would become the largest seaborne invasion in history: the Normandy landings, to liberate France. Some 10,000 American troops arrived in this part of North Devon to practise on a coastline that resembled the French beaches where they were due to land. Here at Baggy Point, troops scaled the cliffs from the sea and used grenades and live fire on dummy pillboxes. The cliff assault practices in particular played a crucial role in the successful capture of the Pointe du Hoc in Normandy, a promontory cliff very similar to Baggy Point.

The coast path continues around the headland, passing an unusual white post with footholds. This is the Baggy Point Coastguard Pole ❹, which was

used in the 20th century to train coastguards to rescue people off ships. The pole is designed to resemble the mast of a sinking ship; the coastguards would fling ropes at it, lassoing them over the top, and then rig up a 'breeches buoy'. This is a kind of life-saver ring on a pulley system, which stricken sailors climb into and are then pulled onto dry land or a rescue vessel. The present pole is a replica erected in 2016, replacing the original which had stood there for around 80 years.

The coast path bears right at the end of the headland, and you start walking east with fantastic views of the sands of Woolacombe and Putsborough ahead and the headland of Morte Point over to the left. The route then turns away from the coast path ❻ and starts to descend back towards Croyde. (If you want to extend the walk to have a swim at Putsborough, simply keep walking on the coast path another 0.6 miles to a lane that leads to the beach).

After leaving the coast path you pass through fields and a small wooded area with a tiny stream,

before following a track past a farm. Approaching the village, the peaceful rural atmosphere starts to dissipate, as you pass an enormous holiday park to the left of the path ❽. Until the 1930s, Croyde was a quiet backwater where the main industry was agriculture, but in the last 100 years, tourism has taken over. The first park – Croyde Bay Holiday Resort, on the southern side of the bay – was created back in 1930 when NALgo, the local government workers' union of the time, bought the site so members had somewhere to go on holiday. It was part of a wider movement by trade unions at the time of the Great Depression to give members a much-needed break. The holiday park is still owned by the union UNISON today, although anyone can stay there.

Once back at the lane, you turn right to make your way back to the car park. On the corner opposite the tea room is an opening which leads directly to the main beach, the perfect opportunity to have a frolic in the surf before heading home.

DIRECTIONS

1 From the car park, turn right into the lane. Fork left following the sign for Baggy Point, and pass the preserved whalebones and the distinctive modern Baggy House. Continue along the coast path, passing Baggy Point Pond on the right. Shortly after the pond, look out for a set of steps on the left.
0.5 miles

2 At the steps, descend to swim in Mermaid's Pool. If the conditions are right, it's possible to swim out of the pool and west along the coast for about 400 metres to find the caves and tunnel **3** following the detailed safety guidelines in the main text. After, rejoin the coast path and continue with the sea on your left. After about 5 minutes' walk, you will find the next swim spot.
0.3 miles

3 You will see a concrete block by the side of the path with a metal cover. From here there is a rough path left down to the rocks; only attempt this path and swim if you are physically strong and confident, and if conditions are completely calm with no swell. Climb down to a sort of rock platform, from which you can scramble along a concrete covered pipe to the rocks. From here, at mid- to high tide, you can swim off the rocks to the left and through a tunnel to the other side. After, retrace your steps to the path and carry on walking with the sea on your left. Follow the coast path around the headland.
0.7 miles

4 You reach the Baggy Point Coastguard Pole. Continue following the path as it bears right and then heads east.
0.4 miles

5 You reach a fork; carry straight on, following the sign for coast path and Woolacombe (if you want to take a short cut back to the car park you can turn right here). Keep following the path through five fields with the sea on your left.
0.6 miles

6 Turn right off the coast path, through a gate, following the sign for Croyde. Walk along the right-hand side of the field downhill through two sets of double gates. After the second set

of gates turn right and walk along the track. Follow it as it turns left by two gates.
0.5 miles

7 You reach a stile between two gates. Climb over it and follow the narrow path, which enters a woody area with a tiny stream by the path. The path emerges at a track with a gate on the right saying 'keep out'. Turn left onto the track and follow it downhill bending left and right, passing farm buildings on the right.
0.7 miles

8 At the lane, turn right and follow the footpath beside the lane back to the car park.
0.2 miles

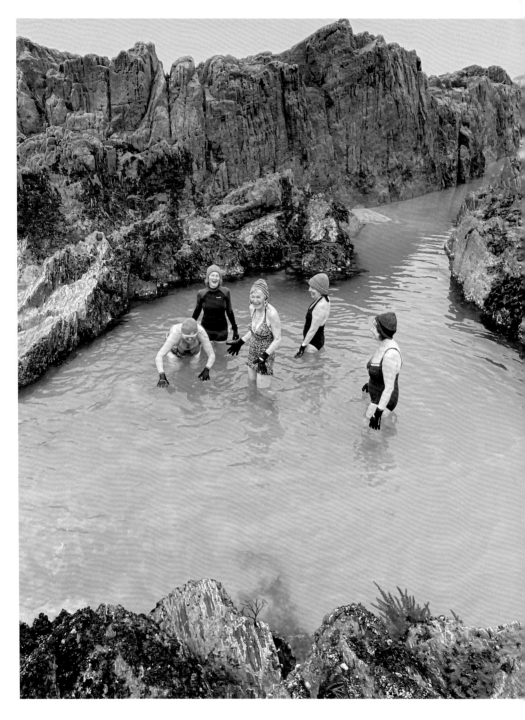

Walk 7

MORTEHOE CIRCULAR

A strenuous hike with spectacular views, taking in an ancient manor, a picturesque village, and swims at several stunning beaches.

INFORMATION

DISTANCE: 8 miles
TIME: Allow all day
MAP: OS Explorer 139 Bideford, Ilfracombe & Barnstaple
START AND END POINT: car park at Mortehoe (SS 457 452, EX34 7DR, What3Words: puts.snowboard.copes)
PUBLIC TRANSPORT: The 31 bus between Ilfracombe and Woolacombe calls at Mortehoe
SWIMMING: Lee Bay (SS 478 465), Sandy Cove (SS 475 467) and Grunta Beach (SS 453 448)
REFRESHMENTS: the Town Farmhouse in Mortehoe serves vegan and vegetarian lunches and cream teas in their garden in the heart of the village (01271 870204, EX34 7DT). The Grampus Inn is a brewpub and small distillery, housed in an ancient building in Lee, which serves craft beers and reasonably priced food, as well as having lots of games including cards and dominoes (01271 862906, EX34 8LR)
EASIER ACCESS: You can drive to Lee Bay, where there is a car park close to the beach; visit at high tide to avoid having to clamber over rocks to reach the water
NEARBY SWIM SPOTS: Barricane Beach, just south of Grunta Beach, is a gorgeous place to swim at high tide and known for its shells. Woolacombe, the next beach down, is famous for its miles of golden sands

The walk starts in the charming village of Mortehoe ❶, which is set back a short distance from the coast, high above the cliffs. Until 1970 it had a railway station, and was one of the stops on the Atlantic Express from Waterloo. This famous service brought visitors to the West Country in their thousands between the 1920s and 1960s, although people had been visiting the area for holidays since the middle of the 19th century.

The route takes you through the village past the Coast-guard Station. The rugged and rocky coastline around here is notorious for shipwrecks, as we shall discover later, but for now we are walking inland, working up to the spectacular journey we'll take around the coast. You leave the village and pass through a campsite, before descending to the intriguingly named Damage Barton ❹, an ancient farmstead which has been owned by the same family since 1962. As well as being a working farm, they also have a campsite nearby. It's thought Damage is the name of the area, (Damage Cliffs are nearby) but no one seems to know the origin of the word.

The route continues down through Borough Woods ❼, which in springtime are packed with primroses and violets. The wood is thought to have been in existence since medieval times, probably because the steep slopes were impossible to develop for agriculture. You walk alongside a pretty stream and arrive in the village of Lee ❽, which is known locally as Fuchsia Valley, because of the profusion of these bright pink and purple flowers in its hedgerows and gardens.

Originally the village was little more than a few houses, occupied by fishermen. But in 1871 local landowner and entre-

preneur Robert Smith decided to prettify it with herringbone stonework walls planted with fuchsias. These flowers have become synonymous with the place, as reported in a 1938 walking guide by countryside campaigner SPB Mais, who describes a visit to "a most attractive tea-garden called Fuchsia Glen. I could not resist the combination of fountain, flowers and running water, so I went into the garden and had a substantial cream tea that I appreciated after my switchback walk over the cliffs."

You'll soon reach the main cove at Lee ❾. There's a rather grand but sad-looking Arts and Crafts building just above the beach, which at the time of writing is derelict, with empty windows and walls overgrown with ivy. This is the Lee Bay Hotel, which was a glamorous place to stay by the sea in its heyday but closed in 2009. Astonishingly, given its incredible position, it has been empty ever since, with developers wanting to knock it down, to local outrage. A new plan has been approved, to convert the building into holiday apartments and build new detached houses and a café on the wider site.

You have various swimming options, depending on the state of the tide. The main beach is very rocky, but if the tide is low, you can walk along a concrete path down the middle of the beach and round to the left, where a lovely bay forms. If it's high, it's probably best to swim at Sandy Cove ⓫, which is further to the left of the main beach. You can walk around to it at low tide, but at other times it's best accessed from the coast path. From the beach at Lee, you head west up the coast road for a short distance, before turning right off onto the coast path. Very soon, on the right, you will see steep steps down to Sandy Cove. Wherever you end up swimming, there are spectacular silvery-grey rock formations to look at and swim around, depending on the state of the tide. These are the Morte Slates, which run in a narrow band from Morte Point (which we will pass later on in the walk) across Devon to Somerset.

The walk continues along the coast path, with spectacular views both east and west, and gets quite tough. You will soon be experiencing the switchback walk described by SPB Mais; the route goes up and down the several steep valleys that occur along this stretch of coastline. You can have a welcome breather at Bennett's Mouth ⑫ delightful little inlet where it's possible to have a swim at high tide. It's very rocky here though, so do take care.

The next point of interest on the walk is Bull Point lighthouse ⑬. There has been a lighthouse here since 1879, but in 1972 the keeper reported alarming ground movement and noticed cracks appearing. A few days later a large section of cliff collapsed into the sea, and the lighthouse (which stood seaward of the cottages) had to be abandoned as it was so dangerous. Two years later, the lighthouse that is still here today was completed. It's now operated remotely, so the accommodation is available for holidays.

The fantastic views just keep on coming as you approach Morte Point. You pass Rockham Bay, a beautiful beach, which until recently, was accessible. Unfortunately, there have been several cliff falls which have resulted in the collapse of the steps down. At the time of writing the National Trust, which manages the area, has no plans to replace them and so sadly this incredible beach is now out of bounds, although some daring souls do manage to scramble down.

You reach Morte Point ⑭, a grand headland from where you can see the beautiful sands of

Woolacombe stretching away to the south. Just off the headland is the Morte Stone, a pinnacle on a mile-long ridge of rocks extending out to sea, where many a ship has foundered. In the 1870s, when the lighthouse was first being planned, many argued for it to be built here rather than along the coast where it ended up.

After rounding the headland, you eventually reach Grunta Beach ⑯. This is covered by the sea at high tide, but you can still swim off the rocks. At low tide it is a glorious stretch of rock pools and channels, many of which are big enough to swim in. We had a wonderful morning exploring in our swimsuits at low tide and spotted some extraordinary marine wildlife in the tidal pools, including green-and-purple snakelocks anemones, as well as orange and green breadcrumb sponges covering the rock faces.

It's a final upwards hike back to Mortehoe, where there are several places to enjoy refreshment before heading home. The church is also worth a visit, with a striking golden mosaic of angels above the chancel arch that makes it feel Byzantine; very unusual in an English church. This is relatively recent: it was commissioned by a local parishioner in memory of his wife and unveiled on Easter Day in 1905. The design is by a notable artist of the time, Selwyn Image, who was also responsible for the 'archangel' window. Workmen previously employed on the mosaics at St Paul's Cathedral executed the scene; the church guidebook ponders how such eminent craftsmen ended up working in a remote Devon church, but does not provide an answer – perhaps the cachet of the artist drew them. There are also some very intricate 13th-century bench ends carved out of chestnut, which are worth seeing.

❶ From the car park, cross the road and continue straight ahead along North Morte Road past the Smugglers Rest on your left and the post office on your right. Continue past the coastguards' office and a sign to Rockham Beach, both on the left. The road starts to ascend; pass the North Morte Farm campsite on the left.
0.3 miles

❷ You reach a junction of paths, with a gate signed for Bull Point Lighthouse on the left. Take the middle path, just to the right of this gate, not the furthest path on the right, and walk through Easewell Farm campsite. Follow the path as it weaves past the Easewell Arms and through the campsite buildings. Pass some ponds and emerge into a field, then onto a gravel path signed 'Public Footpath Lee Bay 1¼

miles'. Continue to follow the path along the field edges.
0.6 miles

❸ You reach a gate and a stile onto a lane. Turn left, following the lane down the hill. You pass a pond on the right and then follow the lane as it bears left and starts gping up hill.
0.2 miles

❹ Bear right around the Damage Barton farm buildings following the footpath sign, and also following signs for Lee Bay and Borough Wood. Follow the path as it turns left away from the farm buildings, and then turn right following the yellow arrows on gates and posts. Bear left through a wooden gate, and pass a rocky outcrop on the left.
0.2 miles

❺ You reach a broken footpath signpost which points to the left. Ignore this and carry straight on, in a south-easterly direction, to reach a footpath sign with a pond ahead and to the right. Bear left at this footpath sign (if you get to the pond you've gone too far), towards another fingerpost you can see in the distance. Go through a gateway and down through two fields.
0.4 miles

❻ Cross a stile which takes you into the road, then another stile opposite into a field. Follow the path down into the woods.
0.3 miles

❼ You reach a T-junction of paths. Go left here, following the sign that says 'Public Footpath to Lee' through a metal kissing gate.

Follow the path downhill with the river on your right. At the bottom cross a footbridge over the river and walk through a field, following the post with a yellow arrow.
0.7 miles

8 At the gate, turn left following the sign for Lee Bay. Cross the river on a small stone bridge and turn right, passing a house called The Gwythers on the left and then public loos on the right.
0.3 miles

9 You arrive at the beach at Lee Bay and can stop for a snack and swim. Return to the road and turn right, with the sea on your right, following the road steeply up the hill.
0.3 miles

10 Just after the speed limit sign, turn right off the road following the National Trust sign for Damage Cliffs. After a short distance the path forks; keep right here. Follow it down to a finger post to Sandy Bay, and follow the steps down to the beach.
0.2 miles

11 After a swim at Sandy Bay, take the steps back up and rejoin the coast path, heading west. Follow the coast path as it ascends and descends through steep valleys.
0.7 miles

12 You reach Bennett's Mouth, a small rocky beach where it's possible to swim with care at high

water. From here continue to follow the coast path with the sea on your right.
0.4 miles

13 You reach Bull Point Lighthouse. Follow the path downhill to the left of the lighthouse, and then continue along the coast path with the sea always on your right. If you are feeling tired, there are a couple of left turns off this section which that take you back to Mortehoe.
1.7 miles

14 You reach Mortehoe Point, with incredible views south to Woolacombe Sands. Continue to follow the coast path around the

headland. As you approach the houses on the cliffs, look for a wooden post-and-rail fence on the edge of the path.
0.8 miles

15 By the fence you will see steps down. Follow these down to Grunta Beach.
0.1 mile

16 At the cove, have a swim and explore the rockpools. Then head back up the steps to the coast path, and follow it uphill and right to where it joins the road. Follow the road back into the village where you started.
0.6 miles

Gannets' Rock, Lundy

Walk 8

LUNDY ISLAND ADVENTURE

An unforgettable day out on an isolated granite island, with a surprising number of swims if you're not averse to clambering up and down a few steep inclines! Take water shoes to protect your feet.

n expedition to Lundy is a proper old-school adventure, starting with the journey out to the wild island itself. During the winter season (start of November to end of March) the only way of getting there is via helicopter from Hartland Point, near Bideford. The exhilarating flight takes just seven minutes, with stunning views over the island and North Devon. In the summer months, the MS *Oldenburg* supply ship and ferry departs several times a week from either Bideford or Ilfracombe and takes around two hours. There are also various charter boats you can book, with some even offering wild swimming tours.

The west side of the island boasts towering, rugged cliffs, but you are likely to approach on the east side. Here the coastline is a bit gentler, with grassy slopes, trees and wild flowers. The island has been called Britain's own Galapagos, due to its remote location and varied habitats with some rare and remarkable wildlife. Ninth-century Vikings are said to have named it, from the Old Norse '*lundi*', meaning puffin; today the island is most famous for these sharply dressed seabirds with their colourful bills, but a large number of other migrating birds also visit in the spring and autumn. The island is also home to around 200 grey seals who you are bound to see, especially at low tide when they like to haul out and rest on the rocks. You may also encounter them when you're in the water; please see the introduction for more information about what to be aware of when swimming with seals.

The island is only 3 miles long and half a mile wide, so we have not created a specific route for this chapter. It is really not necessary,

INFORMATION

GETTING THERE: From the start of April to the end of October the MS Oldenburg ferry runs to Lundy from either Ilfracombe or Bideford. Tickets must be booked in advance (01271 86363 or www.landmarktrust.org.uk/lundyisland/day-trips/). Several companies also run day trips for swimmers; although these cost a little more than a ticket on the main ferry, they will take you to inaccessible coves around the island to swim. We travelled with Lundy Diving (07971 462024, www.lundydiving.co.uk); trips are also provided by Wild Frontier Charters (07447 060036, www.wildfrontiercharters.co.uk) and Ilfracombe Sea Safari (07827 679189, www.ilfracombeseasafari.co.uk). From the beginning of November to end of March there is a helicopter service from Hartland Point (01271 863636)
STAYING ON LUNDY: The island is managed by the Landmark Trust, who have a range of properties to rent all year round (www.landmarktrust.org.uk)
SWIMMING: Devil's Kitchen near the landing place (SS 145 437), Landing Beach (SS 143 437), Quarry Beach (SS 139 450), Brazen Ward (SS 139 468) all year. Jenny's Cove (SS 132 457) and Virgin's Spring (SS 131 481), both out of bounds between 31st March and 14th August because of bird nesting season
REFRESHMENTS: The Marisco Tavern is the island's only pub (01237 431831)
EASIER ACCESS: The Landing Beach is a very short walk from the jetty and you can walk into the water easily

and there are various different things to see and places to go, depending on how much time you have. Instead, we have annotated the map with the swim spots and places of interest, so you can devise your own route according to your own priorities.

If coming by boat, you will arrive at the tiny harbour and jetty at the southern tip of the island. There are immediately two swimming options: one to the left of the jetty, coming from the sea, which is known as Devil's Kitchen ❷, and one to the right, which is Landing Beach ❸. You could try one when you arrive, and the other when you come back to catch the boat home.

To get to the Devil's Kitchen ❷, turn left at the end of the jetty, passing behind a boat shed to scramble down to a beautiful rocky area, overlooked by Rat Island, which dominates the scene, and the much smaller Mouse Island behind it. Rat Island is only an island at high tide, when a lovely, swimmable channel forms between it and the shore; at low the channel empties out to form a beach. Either way, it's a wonderful swim with clear jade water.

Landing Beach ❸ is more obvious, to the right of the jetty on the way up to the village. It's larger and more open than the Devil's Kitchen, and there is handy slipway to enter the water. It's popular with the island's wild swimming group, the Lundy Bluetits, who also like to swim directly off the main jetty when it's clear of boats (which it is for much of the day).

There's a zig-zagging walk up to the village, where the first building you come across is the attractive St Helen's Church ❺. When we visited, they had a chalkboard outside saying 'Prayers at 5pm. Please close the gate to prevent sheep entry'. Inside you will find an exhibition on the history of Lundy and the aptly named Reverend Heaven and

his family, who built the church and many of the buildings. Today, the island has a resident population of about 28 people, including a warden, an island manager, a shopkeeper, maintenance and housekeeping staff, as well as the kitchen and front of house staff at the pub.

You will pass several buildings in the village ❻ including toilets, a small building with an information display and the Lundy General Stores, in a converted 'linhay' barn. This sells supplies for those visiting or staying on the island, as well as Lundy stamps, postcards and supplies for 'letter-boxing', the Lundy variant of geocaching. You will also pass the Marisco Tavern, which operates as a social centre for the staff and visiting guests on the island and is decorated with flotsam and jetsam that has washed up on the shores. The pub is all about socialising and has a ban on mobiles, smartphones and laptops (you'll get a fine if your phone rings in there). There is also no fruit machine, television or amplified music, although acoustic musicians are always welcome to play.

The road continues up past the farm buildings and campsite: where you go from here is very much up to you, and depends on how much time you have on the island. If you are on a day trip, you might just have a couple of hours, while if you are staying, you will obviously be able to explore much more. Pretty much the whole island is open-access land, although we would advise sticking to the paths, so you don't damage any sensitive habitats. You'll pass Highland cows with their dandy fringes and impressive horns, as well as Lundy ponies. Navigation is fairly easy, as the island is crossed by three walls known as Quarter Wall ❾, Halfway Wall ⓭ and Threequarter Wall ⓰.

There are also a few dozen buildings on the island that hint at its many uses in the past. Some

of these are now very quirky holiday lets run by the Landmark Trust. For example, there is a castle with a cottage attached to the keep, three lighthouses, The Old School, The Radio Room, Government House, The Quarters and The Barn, which is a hostel for group bookings. Power is provided by a generator, which is switched off between midnight and 6.00am, making the island particularly good for stargazing. Indeed, the Dark Sky Discovery organisation ranks the island as a 'Milky Way class' site, which means that the Milky Way can be seen with the naked eye. The pub is the only place on the island to have lighting when the generators shut down for the night.

There are a handful of other swimming locations you can head for, depending on how much time and energy you have; they all involve steep climbs down and then back up. The nearest is Quarry Beach ⓬ on the east side of the island. Lundy granite has been quarried for centuries and used to build everything here, from the castle to the church. The Lundy Granite Company was established in 1863 and at its height employed some 200 workers. It ran for almost five years and was responsible for building much of the village, but collapsed due to mismanagement and difficulties in transporting the heavy stone to the mainland.

The cottages that were built for the managers, as well as a hospital, are now picturesque ruins on the cliffs ⓾. The four large quarries that once operated below were connected by a tramway, the remains of which can still be seen. You will also pass the Quarry Pond ⓫ which was one of the earliest cuttings. This could be a swim spot as you make your way down to the beach. Descending the lower path brings you out at the former timekeeper's hut, by a flat area that was part of the tramway; a steep path to the left of this flat area takes you down through ferns and bracken to the beach. This is best swum at high tide, as there are lots of boulders that can be quite hard going to walk over to reach the water.

There are three other swimming places on the island accessible from land: Brazen Ward further up the east coast **17**, Jenny's Cove on the west **15**, and Virgin's Spring on the northern tip by the lighthouse **20**. It's important to note that Jenny's Cove and Virgin's Spring are out of bounds between 31st March and 14th August because of the bird nesting season. You can find out more about the restrictions, including a map showing the exact areas, on the Lundy website (www.landmarktrust.org.uk/lundyisland/discovering-lundy/activities/climbing/).

Brazen Ward is a beautiful spot, again down a steep path, where you can swim off a rocky promontory. It's the site of an early gun battery that may date back to Elizabethan times. You can see the remains of the old buildings, including quite a distinctive old wall.

Jenny's Cove on the western coast can be found close to the Halfway Wall **13**. The cove is named after a three-masted full-rigged ship carrying ivory and gold dust that was wrecked here in 1797. Some of the ivories were apparently later discovered, but the leather bags containing the gold were never found. This used to be an alternative landing place in days gone by, but today it's the main puffin colony; hence the summer restrictions. If you're outside those restrictions, this is a beautifully wild place to swim, although you should only do it in calm conditions. Access is difficult, involving a

scramble down Pyramid Rock, and should only be attempted if you're physically confident. You enter the water from the rocks, admiring the towering cliffs above you, and it feels spectacularly remote.

The final swim spot by the Lundy North Light, Virgin's Spring, is a little cove with a concrete platform you can swim off. There are some steps down to it; again, take care on the steep descent, and remember it too is out of bounds during nesting.

Another fun swimming option for Lundy is to book onto one of the wild swimming tours that are offered by a few boat operators. They cost a little more than the conventional boat fare, but you get taken to inaccessible parts of the island where you can swim off the boat, as well as being dropped off for some time on shore. We travelled with Lundy Diving, who were really welcoming and full of fascinating anecdotes about the area; they took us to Gannets' Bay **18** at the north-eastern tip of the island, where we had fun swimming in the crystal-clear waters and enjoying the sights of seals and a pretty islet called Gannets' Rock **19**.

As you get on the boat to start the crossing back to the mainland, think what it would be like to swim across instead. The first attempt was in 1952: Egyptian channel swimmer Hassan Abdel Rehim succeeded, swimming alongside Cyril Webber, who unfortunately had to abandon the attempt because of sea sickness. There was then a long gap until 2010, when lifeguard and surf coach Nick Thorn swam from Lundy to Woolacombe – about 20 miles. Then in 2017, Steve Maclure and Gary Readman swam from Hartland to Lundy, a distance of about 15 miles. Most recently, Sadie Davies swam from Hartland to Lundy in 2019, becoming the first woman to do so. Hopefully there will be more epic swims to Lundy in future, but for now, enjoy the boat trip, and look out for dolphins!

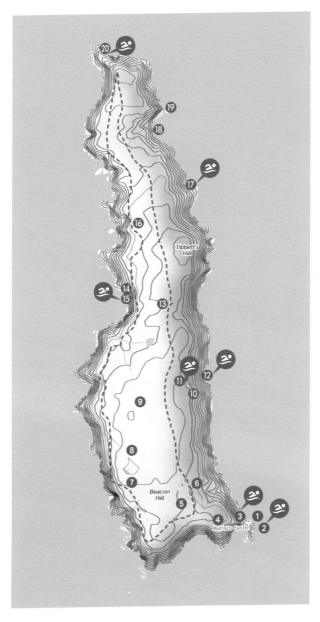

1. Landing Place
2. Devil's Kitchen
3. Landing Beach
4. Ruins of castle
5. St Helen's Church
6. Village centre – pub, shop and museum
7. Cemetery
8. Airstrip
9. Quarter Wall
10. Quarry buildings
11. Pond
12. Quarry Beach
13. Halfway Wall
14. The Pyramid
15. Jenny's Cove (closed in nesting season)
16. Threequarter wall
17. Brazen Ward
18. Gannets' Bay
19. Gannets' Rock
20. Virgin's Spring (closed in nesting season)

Walk 9

ILFRACOMBE AND HELE BAY

A bracing walk from the harbour up over Hillsborough Nature Reserve, with several wonderful swim spots along the way. For optimum swimming visit during the top half of the tide. If you have time, we highly recommend a visit to the legendary Tunnels Beaches while you are in the area; these are best visited at low water.

INFORMATION

DISTANCE: 3 miles (3.5 miles with visit to Tunnels Beach)
TIME: Allow 4 hours with stops and swims
MAP: OS Explorer 139 Bideford, Ilfracombe & Barnstaple
START AND END POINT: Ropery car park (SS 522 477, EX34 9EF What3Words: insisting.inserted.retain)
PUBLIC TRANSPORT: Ilfracombe is pretty well served by buses including the 301 from Combe Martin, 31 from Woolacombe, 21 from Westward Ho, Bideford and Barnstaple, and 33 from Berrynarbor
SWIMMING: Rapparee Cove (SS 528 477), Hele Bay (SS 535 478), Tunnels Beaches bonus swim (SS 514 477)
REFRESHMENTS: The Bay Café at Hele Bay is a fantastic dog-friendly venue with outside seating right by the beach (01271 863911, EX34 9QZ). Hele Corn Mill and Tea Room opens from March to October and is a working mill where they make their own flour, used in some delicious baked goodies; dogs are allowed in the tea garden (01271 863185, EX34 9QY)
EASIER ACCESS: You can park in the road right next to Hele Bay, from where it's a short walk down the slipway into the sea
NEARBY SWIM SPOTS: Sandy Bay, just west of Lee Bay, is a lovely spot to swim at high water

Today's walk starts at the pretty harbour area of Ilfracombe ❶, where the fishing boats rest on the sand on a low tide. You can't possibly miss Damien Hirst's controversial sculpture *Verity*, which people either love or hate. Standing 20 metres tall, she looks out over the Bristol channel and has two sides to her. From St Nicholas' Chapel on Lantern Hill, you see simply a pregnant woman holding a sword aloft in one hand and the scales of justice in the other. From the quay, you can see her internal anatomy, including her skull and the foetus inside her. It's as Marmite as a piece of art can be, but it gets people talking.

Good news for swimmers is that North Devon councillors have agreed to create a new seawater pool right next to Verity. It will be in an enclosed area in the rocks that fills up at high tide, and has railings alongside; some locals are swimming there already. A brand-new Community Watersports Centre has also opened at Larkstone Cove – across the water from *Verity* – behind which the walk passes as it heads up the hill away from the harbour. This has storage for boats, a slipway offering easy access to the water and a brand-new café with stunning views, further helping to regenerate the town.

Ilfracombe has a long history of welcoming swimmers, and the first beach we drop down to, Rapparee Cove ❹ was one of the most popular bathing beaches in its Victorian heyday. Steep steps lead down to the beach, where there is sand on a lower tide, and

high cliffs protect the cove from all but onshore winds, making it perfect for swimming. Once there would have been bathing huts and a regular ferry service down here, and there is still a Victorian shelter. You may well bump into some local wild swimmers who enjoy this safe, quiet and picturesque spot for a dip.

You pass a memorial stone on your way down to the beach, commemorating a ship called London that sank off the cove in 1796. Upwards of 40 bodies are buried below the cliffs here, many of them losing their lives because they were chained below deck; several local people also perished in the storms attempting to rescue them. There's some debate whether they were enslaved Africans from St Lucia and bound for Bristol, or French prisoners. Gold and silver coins have been found

in the area, and Ilfracombe Dive Club has visited the wreck on numerous occasions, bringing back items including cannonballs.

The beach was also once the setting of an international diplomatic incident, when Prince Frederick William of Prussia, the future German Kaiser, visited Ilfracombe as a teenager in 1878. He started hurling stones at beach huts and the holidaymakers in them and was confronted by a young local beach hut attendant called Alfie Price. The prince called him a peasant and ordered him to back down, but Alfie told his aristocratic adversary "I don't care a dash who you are – stop chucking stones or it will be the worse for you." A clash ensued, in which Alfie floored the prince in a single blow, giving the future emperor a bloody nose. Apparently, the future German leader's entourage later paid Alf thirty bob to keep quiet, which was quite a large sum at the time.

It has been suggested that the incident may explain the famous hatred of the British felt by 'Kaiser Bill', even though his grandmother was Queen Victoria; his aggressive policies would later contribute to the onset of the First World War. A comic poem called 'Why the Kaiser Hates England. Or, What Happened at Rapparee' was written by WH Coates in 1916 and circulated amongst British soldiers to boost morale; it can be seen in the archives at Ilfracombe Museum along with various press cuttings, and includes a threat from the prince:

Mine friend! You'll rue this day
For what you've done t'mine poor nose.
Mine word! I'll make you pay,
I'll build big ships and gurt big guns,
Then one day I will come
And blow this place t'smithereens
And you..............t'kingdom come.

The walk continues from the other end of the beach and up onto Hillsborough, a local nature reserve. It's known locally as the sleeping elephant, as that's what it looks like when viewed from Ilfracombe Harbour. If you are feeling energetic, you can also hike up to the ramparts of an Iron Age hillfort ❺, which is around 2,000 years old. It's the largest cliff castle in the south-west, and its strategic position commands spectacular views of the north Devon coast, Exmoor National Park, the Bristol Channel and the south Wales coastline. Interestingly, the whole Hillsborough area is one of the earliest examples of countryside conservation in the country, being was purchased by Ilfracombe Urban District Council in 1895 to prevent it being built upon.

You will also enjoy great views back down to Ilfracombe and St Nicholas' Chapel at the entrance to the harbour. Dating back to the 14th century, the chapel was named after the patron saint of sailors, and since the 15th century it has housed a beacon to guide shipping into the harbour, making it the oldest working lighthouse in the UK. Today it is maintained by Trinity House (who look after all of the lighthouses around Britain) and looked after by the Rotarians. To the left you will also spot the iconic Landmark Theatre with its distinctive double-cone roof, known to locals as 'Madonna's Bra'.

The walk continues through woods before dropping down a very steep path to Hele Bay ❼. This was a haven for smugglers in the 18th and 19th centuries, when the 'gentlemen of the night' would land their contraband here, including brandy, gin, tea and anything else that was subject to import duties. Later, coal was landed on the beach (you can still see the mooring post) and taken by cart up Beach Road, to be used for the

production of gas at the works that opened here in 1905. Children would collect discarded lumps of coal from the beach, while women would use the small stream to wash clothes. However, when the steam whistle called the men to work, the women quickly removed the clothes from the water, as black smuts would wash down from the coal burning.

The gas works closed in 1963 and the holiday parks moved in. The area above the beach used to be covered in static caravans; these have now been replaced by small holiday lodges that look like beach huts and have enviable views over the bay. It's a fantastic spot for swimming, with a slipway providing good access to the water, and handy stone arches under which you can change. On a low tide it's also great for rockpooling, while on a really low tide you can clamber over rocks on the left to reach Fishing Rock or Blythe's Cove. There used to be a path down to this cove, named after Captain Blythe, a prominent local gentleman who enjoyed bathing there throughout all four seasons towards the end of the 19th century.

While taking a dip you may stumble across the Hele Bay Merbabes, a wonderfully supportive group formed in 2019. Open to men as well as women (anyone can be a babe), it now has more than a thousand members. If you're a bit cold after your dip, you'll soon warm up as you make your way back up the steep hill the way you came, before turning off to walk around the inland side of the Hillsborough hillfort. It's then a picturesque drop down back towards the harbour area, where we think a portion of fish and chips – or whatever takes your fancy – would be in order.

TUNNELS BEACHES

We highly recommend visiting Tunnels Beaches when you are in Ilfracombe: they offer not only a swim in a Victorian seawater pool but also a fascinating insight into the history of swimming for health. They are about 15 minutes' walk westwards from the harbour, with a modest entry fee to help maintain the town's most popular attraction. As the name suggests, you walk down to the shore through a series of tunnels, which were hand carved by Welsh miners in the 1820s. Along the way you can read some fascinating information boards about the history of the place, with evocative black and white images. There are also hilarious guides to Victorian etiquette for boys, girls and "when boating with the ladies."

You first arrive at the Beach Venue, which is now one of the most popular places in the town for weddings. It houses a rather lovely restaurant (which can be used on non-wedding days) with stunning views over the former Gentleman's Bathing Beach below. More tunnels take you past changing facilities and a beach shop that sells refreshments and out onto the Ladies' Bathing Beach. This has the only remaining tidal pool still open from the original three; there are plans to restore the Gentleman's Pool in the future.

The Ladies' Pool is a wonderful place to swim, and these days gentleman are allowed in too. Back in the days of segregated bathing, if a man was caught approaching from the gentleman's pool to spy on the ladies, a bugler would blow an alarm call and the man would be arrested. A little bit of planning is required, as the pool is visible for three hours before and after low tide. It's a magical spot for a dip, with fascinating rock formations in the Bristol Channel behind the pool.

The area is also amazing for rockpooling and was made world famous in Victorian times by Philip Henry Gosse, a renowned biologist and friend of Darwin. He discovered several new species here, causing an influx of visitors eager to enjoy shell-collecting and rockpooling. The huge tidal range also means you can see some very unusual species on a low tide, including rare sea corals. On the way out, we highly recommend purchasing a copy of the souvenir booklet, which is packed with quirky history, amazing anecdotes and some fantastic old pictures. You will also be supporting this wonderful historic institution for future generations to enjoy.

DIRECTIONS

1 From Ropery car park, look for Adele's café on the corner of Broad Street and Hiern's Lane, and head down Hiern's Lane to the harbour. Once at the harbour, bear right and follow the quay, walking with the harbour on your left. Continue along the road.
0.4 miles

2 You reach a bridge on your left; cross it and immediately turn left up some steps which take you into a car park. Bear right across the car park and exit through a gate at the end on the right by a building with a sign for golf on it. Bear left. Do not follow the path uphill to the right across the golf course (if you do this you will miss Rapparee Cove), but continue bearing left, looking ahead for a small post with a yellow arrow on it.
0.1 mile

3 At the post with the yellow arrow, walk downhill and bear right. Follow the path down to the beach.
0.1 miles

4 You arrive at Rapparee Cove. After a dip, take the path at the eastern end of the beach and continue along the coast path with the sea on your left, following signs for Hele Bay.
0.2 miles

5 You arrive at a path to the right with a sign for the hillfort, and can make a short diversion up here if you wish. After, return to the main coast path and continue walking with the sea on your left. The path ascends and then descends, passing a wonderful viewpoint back to Ilfracombe. You enter a wood, going downhill. Ignore the first path off to the right and keep on towards the sea.
0.4 miles

6 You reach another spectacular viewpoint, with views back to Ilfracombe and over towards Hele. From here, follow the path as it doubles back and continues downhill and then down steps.
0.3 miles

7 You reach Hele Bay. Stop here for another dip, then leave the beach the way you came, back up the steps.
0.1 mile

8 Take the first left after ascending from the beach and follow the path along the side of the hill. Ignore paths joining from the right.
0.3 miles

9 You reach a fork with two gates on the left. Take the right-hand fork, heading uphill. Keep going straight, ignoring a gateway to the left, which leads to the swimming pool below. Keep going straight on.
0.2 miles

10 You reach a crossroads of paths. Turn left here, following the sign for Ilfracombe. You emerge at the top of the golf course. Head downhill to the left, and head back into town the way you came.
0.6 miles

Walk 10

WATERMOUTH AND BROADSANDS CIRCULAR

A short but at times challenging walk to one of the most photographed beaches in Devon, with adventurous swims around two tiny tidal islands. Take swim shoes to protect your feet; the walk is best done around high tide.

The walk starts in Watermouth Harbour ❶, an attractive U-shaped bay flanked either side by long arms of rock. It forms a perfect pool for swimmers when the tide is in. Philip Gosse described it in his 1853 book *A Naturalist's Rambles on the Devonshire Coast* as "a very romantic creek, being walled in as it were by high precipitous rocks, especially at the very mouth, one side of which is formed by a conical hill, gay with blooming furze."

The walk is best done two hours either side of high water for optimum swimming, although you can get in at all states of the tide; you just have more options at high. You can swim straight from the harbour, but we prefer to walk along to the end of the northern arm of the cove, near its mouth. The route takes you past an unusual building called the Round Tower, about which very little is known. Historic England says it is "probably a look-out associated with Watermouth Castle", a 19th-century country house just behind the harbour. On old maps it is marked as a 'pleasure house', so we prefer to think it was built by the castle owners as an upmarket beach hut where they could take tea (or something stronger) and warm up after an invigorating dip.

At the end of the headland, just past the Round Tower, a small fishermen's path on the left ❷ leads through blackthorn bushes down to the shore, where there is an old set of steps carved into the rocks. At high water, you can swim directly off these steps. It's the perfect launching point for an adventurous swim around the islet of Sexton's Burrow at the mouth of the harbour, the 'conical hill' mentioned by Gosse. Of course, it goes without saying that

INFORMATION

DISTANCE: 3 miles
TIME: 3 hours
MAP: OS Explorer 139 Bideford, Ilfracombe & Barnstaple
START AND END POINT: car park at Watermouth Harbour (SS 555 481, EX34 9SJ, What3Words: else. hologram.shift)
PUBLIC TRANSPORT: The 301 bus between Combe Martin, Ilfracombe and Barnstaple calls at Watermouth Bay
SWIMMING: Sexton's Burrow (SS 551 484) and Broadsands Beach (SS 563 478), both best at high tide
REFRESHMENTS: Storm in a Teacup is a lovely café in Watermouth Cove, which does particularly good cheese scones (07846 496069, EX34 9SJ). The Sawmills Inn/Freehouse is conveniently situated towards the end of the walk and serves pub grub like burgers and nachos (01271 883388, EX34 9SJ)
EASIER ACCESS: At high water Watermouth Harbour is directly accessible from the car park. Unfortunately, Broadsands is only accessible via a long, steep staircase with over 200 steps
NEARBY SWIM SPOTS: Combe Martin is a fun place for a dip, and Wild Pear Beach to the east of Combe Martin is a stunning, unspoilt bay only accessible on foot, with a very steep final descent

you need calm, still conditions, as there are a lot of rocks; do not attempt this route in surf and swell.

From the steps, turn right, swimming towards the open sea. On the right, you'll soon pass a channel between the islet and the shore. Keep going and bear right around the seaward side of Sexton's Burrow, where you will soon find a really beautiful lagoon you can swim into on your right. At this point you have two options: you can either swim to the inner end of the lagoon and get out on the rocks to clamber to the channel on the other side, or you can swim back out of the lagoon and carry on around Sexton's Burrow and then bear right into the channel. Either way, once in the channel you can swim back to the steps. This makes a wonderful mini-adventure, with the satisfaction you get from swimming around an island, however small! On a calm day, with a still sea, it is an absolutely beautiful experience, as the cliffs tower above you and the sea teems with seaweed and fish below.

If you don't fancy the circuit around the islet, it is still really good fun to swim into the channel that separates it from the mainland (and which empties out at low tide). Or for another challenge, you could swim across to the beach on the other side.

Today, pretty much the only activity you'll see in the harbour is boating, but in the past it was busy with both fishermen and smugglers. Rumour has it that there used to be a smugglers' tunnel leading inland from the beach, which has since been blocked up. In Victorian times, fishermen would string nets across the harbour to catch grey mullet, with reports of two hundredweight of fish being taken on one tide alone. Now it is purely a place of recreation.

After your swim, retrace your steps back to the harbour. In the distance, you will see the fairytale vision of Watermouth Castle, which overlooks the sea. With its crenellations and turrets, it gives a romantic feel to this very pretty part of the coast. It was built in 1825 in the Gothic style by the Basset family, who owned it and the nearby village of Berrynarbor for well over a century. It is now a theme park and tourist attraction which, at the time of writing, had just been sold for the first time in nearly 50 years. The new owners, the Escapade Group, plan to keep it as a holiday resort.

The walk continues for a very short distance on the main road before turning off to the left ❸, and ascending through a campsite. If you walk to the seaward edge of the field, you will be rewarded with superb views both up and down the coast, and to the left, you will see the main campsite complex. There is a set of caves which used to be a public attraction; in Victorian times people would pay a few pence to go and visit them. Sadly this is no longer possible, unless you take a boat into the cove or are staying at the campsite.

As you ascend through the camping field, the coast path bears right. Keep a look out for a spectacular viewpoint at the top, with a bench so you can relax and take it in. It looks down over Broadsands Beach, our next swim spot, called by some the 'Is it really in England?' beach, and by others 'Little Thailand'. When the sun is shining (and even when it's not), it could be a scene in Vietnam or some other part of south-east Asia: the sea is a wonderful shade of green and forms a beautiful curve against the beach, with conical rocks in both the foreground and the distance framing the scene. You'll be itching to get down there, but there's a bit more walking to do first.

You follow the route for a short way along the coast path, before starting the steep descent to Broadsands ❺. There are over 200 steps down, but the views of the sea through the trees are magical. Once down on the beach, you'll want to rest and then swim, and there is a veritable maze of caves and channels to explore.

On the right-hand side is Hamator Rock, which becomes an island at high tide, and you can swim right around it via the channel that separates it from the main shoreline. It is also fun to swim south-east along the coast towards Combe Martin, from where there are wonderful views across to Wild Pear Beach on the other side of the bay. In the other direction, on the left-hand side of the beach, there are numerous caves that you can swim or climb up to, depending on the state of the tide. It really is an enchanting place.

Less enchanting is the climb back up to the coast path. The steps are steep, and you will feel every single one. It was while we were about halfway up that we decided this would be our last wild swimming walks guide. This climb was the last straw!

Once at the top, retrace your steps for a short distance, but do not return to the coast path (unless you want to go back the way you came). Instead, follow the route downhill along a wide driveway. This used to be the old coast road, but in the 1920s it became badly eroded and fell out of use. You pass a campsite called Napps, which occupies an area which was once extensively quarried, for limestone in particular. In the early 1900s some miners broke into a natural pothole, which they discovered led into an extensive system of caves and tunnels, containing large clusters of rare aragonite crystal stalactites. Although mining stopped in 1912, specimens from the cave were sold to visiting tourists for some years after.

You reach the main coast road and turn right, passing the Sawmills pub ❻. This building operated as a sawmill until 1933, and the waterwheel was used to supply electricity to nearby Watermouth Castle. It is now a handy place for a pitstop if you feel in need of refreshment. The walk continues down the road and back to the harbour, where you can have a last swim if you wish.

DIRECTIONS

1 From Watermouth Harbour, looking at the sea, bear right across a footbridge over a stream, following the path as it turns left along the northern arm of the cove. Pass the Round Tower and continue until you reach the end and are looking over a channel to the islet of Sexton's Burrow. Turn around and look back.
0.4 miles

2 You will see a small path off to the right. Scramble down onto the rocks, from which you can climb down to the water or the beach (depending on the state of the tide). Stop here for a swim around Sexton's Burrow, then retrace your steps to the harbour and walk up the road out of the harbour and through a gate to the main road.
0.5 miles

3 At the road, turn left, then shortly after the campsite entrance, left again on a footpath crossing a bridge over a river. Follow the path into the campsite and then bear right uphill. At the top, on the left, look for a great viewpoint down to Broadsands.
0.4 miles

4 You reach a gate in a wall. Turn left here.
0.1 miles

5 Turn left down a path with a sign saying 'Broadsands Beach'. Follow the steep steps all the way down to the beach. After a swim, take the steps back to the top and retrace your steps to point 4. Do

not turn right through the gate (unless you want to go back as you came and avoid walking on the road) but carry on straight ahead, following the lane down the hill to the main road.
0.7 miles

6 At the main road, turn right and follow the path alongside the road all the way back to point 3 and down to the harbour.
0.7 miles

Walk 11

HEDDON'S MOUTH
AND WOODY BAY

This is a challenging and beautiful walk up, down and along the famous hog's-back cliffs of this part of Devon, with swims at two stunning beaches. Take water shoes to protect your feet; the swims are best done at high water, although both beaches are swimmable at low.

INFORMATION

DISTANCE: 8 miles
TIME: Allow all day
MAP: OS Explorer OL9 Exmoor
START AND END POINT: Hunters Inn National Trust car park (SS 655 480, EX31 4PY, What3Words: informal.successor.drags)
PUBLIC TRANSPORT: None; the nearest bus is the 309 between Barnstaple and Lynton is which stops at Martinhoe Cross
SWIMMING: Heddon's Mouth (SS 654 495), Woody Bay (SS 677 489) both best around high water, although both swimmable at all states of the tide
REFRESHMENTS: National Trust café by the car park serves the usual drinks and snacks (EX31 4PY). The Hunter's Inn, also by the car park, serves pub classics in a more formal setting (01598 763230, EX31 4PY)
EASIER ACCESS: the route down to Heddon's Mouth is maintained by the National Trust as a tramper-friendly route, but at the beach there is still a climb down over rocks and boulders to reach the water
NEARBY SWIM SPOTS: Combe Martin has a lovely beach, which is particularly good at high water

A century ago, the famous 'red guides' published by Ward Lock gave "amusing and readable" introductions to destinations all over Europe. The author of the guide to north-west Devon declared "The scenery in this district is generally considered the most romantic in Devon, and it is impossible to overpraise it." And they were right. The Heddon Valley, where we start the walk, is in the cleft of a beautiful, wooded combe, which has been popular with visitors for many years. Make sure you have plenty of water and decent walking boots, as this is one of the hardest walks in the book, being around 8 miles long and with over 600 metres of ascent. If you're not feeling that energetic, you can just do the first part, down to Heddon's Mouth for a swim and then back.

The first point of interest is the Hunter's Inn, which you pass soon after leaving the car park ❶. It was built in its present form in 1906; before this it was a thatched cottage, whose tenants used to supply beer to local shooting parties. This burnt down in 1895 and was rebuilt by an entrepreneur called Benjamin Lake in an Arts and Crafts half-timbered style, which was very fashionable at the time. It was designed to resemble a Swiss chalet; at the time the area had been dubbed 'Little Switzerland' by tourism supremos, keen to market its dramatic scenery. The hotel is now owned by the National Trust, and profits are used to support conservation in the area.

The route heads down towards the sea, alongside the tumbling River Heddon ❷ which is home to brown trout. The whole valley is an SSSI because of its wildlife includes otters and the rare high brown fritillary. The name Heddon is derived from eoten, the Old English for giant, and this dramatic cleave certainly conjures up the idea of ancient monsters. Funnily enough, a theatre group performed a story walk down the valley to the sea in 2013, and the tale they told was *Hunting the Giant's Daughter*.

You reach a small wooden footbridge ❷, which you cross to the other side of the river. As you walk, you'll notice how steep the walls of the valley are. They're over 200 metres high, with a gradient of seven in ten. They are very bare, particularly on the western side, and there are large areas of scree. These were created during the last Ice Age, when the permafrost at the top of the cliffs thawed and sent a flow of loose rock down the steep sides of the valley.

You arrive at the beach ❸, where there is an old lime kiln on the western side, which was restored by the National Trust in 1982. It was built in the 18th century to receive limestone and coal shipped over from south Wales; the last load was delivered about 1870, after which it fell into disuse.

The cliffs towering above the shore are some of the highest in England. It is a wonderfully dramatic place to swim, with channels and islets on both sides of the main beach that are fun to explore when the sea is calm. On a sunny, still day the water is very clear, because there is no sand. When we visited the colours were entrancing: turquoise sea with patches of acid-bright green seaweed on the rocks below the surface.

Like many remote coves, Heddon's Mouth was the haunt of smugglers in time past. There are even stories of Nazi U-boats stopping here during the Second World War to stock up with fresh water

from the river. Whatever the stories, it is an idyllic spot to swim and relax.

After some time on the beach, the route returns along the river before crossing back over and starting a big climb up to the top of the cliffs. The path takes you through woods, which peter out as you get higher, and you are rewarded with dramatic views over to the other side of the valley and back down to Heddon's Mouth. You reach an impressive rocky promontory called Highveer Point ❻ which is directly above the eastern side of the beach. This is one of the largest and most spectacular headlands along this part of the coast. There is a wonderful description of it by SH Burton in his book *Exmoor*: "The impression from the summit of Highveer is … of a starkly magnificent desolation: a wild antiquity made the wilder by the ruins of the limekiln on the western bank, so dignified by decay that they look like the remains of some stronghold." This was obviously written before the lime kiln was restored!

Continue to walk east along the top of the cliffs, with great views both north and south, including of a beautiful natural arch. You then pass a large waterfall ❼ lined with bright green mosses and other flora. This is one of several along the course of the Hollow Brook, which eventually disappears down over the cliff to the shore in is a final waterfall, only visible by boat.

The route then descends through West Woodybay Wood, which is full of sessile oak trees, bent by the wind into fantastical shapes. It's awash with bluebells in late spring. At this point you will start to see tantalising glimpses of the red cliffs of Woody Bay, our next swim stop.

The path joins a road ❽ which then becomes a track all the way down to Woody Bay ❾. The fact that there's a road at all is thanks to the entrepreneur who rebuilt the Hunter's Inn, Benjamin Lake. He owned the land between there and Woody Bay, and thought the latter would be the perfect place to develop a new tourist resort, so he had a carriageway built to take holidaymakers between the two; our route back will take us along this. There were even ambitious plans for a cliff railway, like the one at nearby Lynton, but they never came to fruition.

As you near the final descent to the beach, a small path diverts off to the left. If you follow it down you will find a dead end, a sort of lookout, and if you look over you will see the remains of a jetty. This was another of Lake's grand plans, built so that paddle steamers, which were popular at the time, could call at Woody Bay. The stone jetty was opened in 1897 but was not a success, with many ships unable to dock because it was too short to be used at all states of the tide. It was then badly hit by storms and ended up being demolished by locals in 1902.

However, one thing built by Lake does remain – a tidal pool. Once you're down on the beach, stand in the middle and you will see a large protruding rock. The pool is just to the right of it, created between it and another large rock. A solid wall retains the water when the tide goes out; you can see it is Victorian because it is solidly built out of blocks of stone, rather than being made of concrete like most such pools around the coast. Of course, much of the infrastructure has now gone, but it does still function.

Woody Bay is a truly beautiful spot, with steep cliffs encircling the small bay, and a waterfall called, unsurprisingly, Hanging Water. You can understand why Lake wanted to develop it, and if it wasn't for him, we probably wouldn't be able to access it today. Sadly, his career ended in bankruptcy, and he was sent to prison.

After a refreshing swim, you start the long and steep walk back up to the top of the cliffs, and head back along the carriageway. Again, you are rewarded with spectacular views. You pass a large rocky crag called the Beacon ⑪ behind which there are the remains of a Roman fortlet. There is a little path off to the left where you can climb up to have a look, although to be honest, there is not much to see. It is clearer in aerial photos, where you can see the small, square outline of the fortlet and a larger circular enclosure teetering on the edge of the cliffs. It is really quite incredible to think there was a small outpost of the Roman empire here, built to guard the north Devon coast. It's thought it was established in the 1st century AD, and the buildings would have been made of wood; about a hundred Roman soldiers would have been based here, under the command of the Second Augustan legion based at Exeter. It was excavated in the 1960s, and archaeologists found a plate as well as cooking pots and other items.

Shortly after passing the fortlet, the route (thankfully) starts to descend and you make your way back down to rejoin the path in the woods you originally set out on. It's definitely time to rest your feet and seek refreshment in the inn or the café before heading home!

DIRECTIONS

1 From the car park, turn left down the road towards Hunter's Inn. In front of the inn, bear right and then turn immediately left along the track to the right of the inn, signed 'Public Bridleway Heddon's Mouth and Woody Bay'. Very soon the path forks; bear left, following the path as it ascends and then descends, with the river on your left.
0.6 miles

2 You reach a stone bridge. Cross the river to the other side and continue walking with the river on your right, passing a footbridge.
0.6 miles

3 You reach Heddon's Mouth. Stop for a swim and then retrace your steps to the footbridge.
0.2 miles

4 Cross the footbridge and turn right, walking with the river on your right.
0.3 miles

5 Turn left, uphill, following the sign for Coast Path and Woody Bay. You're now starting a steep ascent.
0.4 miles

6 You reach Highveer Point, a great headland from where you can look back down to Heddon's Mouth. Continue to follow the coast path as it heads east, with the sea on your left.
0.7 miles

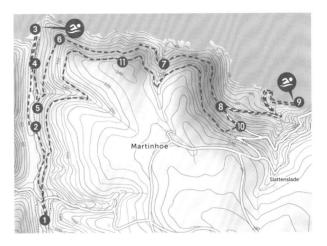

Martinhoe

Slattenslade

7 You pass a large waterfall on your right. Keep following the coast path as it enters the woods.
0.6 miles

8 You reach a junction with a road; turn left here, going downhill. You pass a signpost pointing to Iceland, Russia, America and New Zealand, and a sign on the left for Martinhoe Manor. Follow the road all the way to Woody Bay.
0.9 miles

9 At Woody Bay, have a swim. Then retrace your steps all the way back up the road to point 8 (where you joined from the footpath). Do not go back on the footpath, but bear left on the road, continuing to walk uphill. Pass Wringapeak House on your right. Very shortly after this look for a footpath to your right. The sign is low, so be careful you don't miss it.
0.9 miles

10 Turn right onto the footpath which is signposted Martinhoe ½. This is a very steep climb up a narrow and uneven path. (If it is too much you can continue along the road until a T junction where you can then hairpin turn right and then pick up the route; this is a longer, but less steep ascent). At the top of the steep path, you meet a track which is the old Victorian carriageway. Turn right here.
1.2 miles

11 You pass a large crag, site of a Roman fortlet. Keep walking on the coast path, which eventually starts to descend back towards Heddon Valley. The path joins with the one you started on near Hunter's Inn, and from there you retrace your steps back to the car park.
1.6 miles

Walk 12

PORLOCK WEIR AND CULBONE CHURCH

A spectacular walk from the pretty port of Porlock Weir, following a route up through verdant woodlands to a remote church in a quiet, shaded combe. Swimming on this walk is only possible at high tide, so time your walk accordingly.

This walk starts at the picturesque port of Porlock Weir ❶, which has offered safe harbour where the lush green hills of Exmoor tumble down to the sea for more than 1,000 years. Charming stone buildings and thatched cottages surround the harbour, including the Ship Inn, which dates back to the 15th century, and the Porlock Weir Hotel. It's an ideal place to pick up supplies and browse some of the shops – or do what we did and go for a dip in the harbour to get the day started in the best possible way. It's important to note that swimming here is only possible at high water; at low water the harbour dries out.

You can either enter the water from the pebbles directly in front of the hotel or make your way over to the café, turn right and cross the lock gates to the pretty 17th-century Gibraltar Cottages on what is known as Turkey Island. Look out for the Second World War pillbox, which has been battered by wind and tides and now rests at a lopsided angle with what looks like an expression of surprise upon its face. You can enter the water here by the weather-beaten wooden groynes, which extend the quay wall along the pebble beach. This is where many local swimmers get in, and you will usually find someone swimming here at high tide. We swam amongst the pleasure craft, although be aware that if a boat is coming in or leaving you should stay behind the long sticks in the water – called withies – that mark the main channel, leaving the channel clear for boats.

Looking out to sea you will spot Hurlstone Point off to the right and the waters known for the famous Porlock Bay oysters. Indeed,

INFORMATION

DISTANCE: 6 miles
TIME: Allow all day
MAP: OS Explorer Map OL 9 Exmoor
START AND END POINT: Car park at Porlock Weir (SS 864 479, TA24 8PB, What3Words: howler.rapid.registers)
PUBLIC TRANSPORT: The 10 bus runs between Minehead and Porlock Weir Monday to Saturday. The nearest mainline train station is Taunton (28 miles away), from where you would need to get a bus to Minehead and change to the 10 for Porlock Weir
SWIMMING: The harbour at Porlock Weir (SS 864 479) at the start and/or end of your walk. Swimming is only possible at high tide, so time your walk around that.
REFRESHMENTS: The Harbour House Coffee Shop is really welcoming and dog friendly, with great harbour views and some delicious cakes (TA24 8PD). The Ship Inn (Bottom Ship) serves local ales, lagers and cider, as well as pub grub (01642 863288, TA24 8PB)
NEARBY SWIM SPOTS: Lynmouth is very pretty and there's a strong community of swimmers there; you will usually find someone swimming at high tide.
EASIER ACCESS: The harbour is very close to the car park, although the beach is quite pebbly, so might prove tricky for those with limited mobility.

the coast here is so clean, it is one of only a handful of sites across the UK to boast category A waters, where the finest oysters thrive on the plankton carried in by the tides.

Porlock comes from the old English 'port loca' meaning an enclosure near a harbour. The weir part comes from the stone and hazel fishing weirs that were once common here. These were basically curved walls that trapped fish as the tide went out and kept them alive until they were harvested. It's believed that the arms of these traps were once at least 130 metres long. The Bristol Channel has the highest tidal range in Britain, which would have helped the process; at Porlock Weir, the range between the high and low tide can be in excess of 10 metres.

A path leads up between the Ship Inn and the Porlock Weir Hotel, and you are soon in fields with views across the Bristol Channel to Wales. The walk rises to Worthy Combe Toll Lodge ❷, which was once the lodge for Ashley Combe House. It was built in the late 19th century in the Arts and Crafts style and is very picturesque. Continuing up the path, you encounter two short tunnels that were once part of an Italian garden belonging to Ashley Combe House. Built in 1799 as a hunting lodge, this became the summer retreat of Ada Lovelace, the gifted mathematician and daughter of Lord Byron, and her husband, the engineer Lord William King, the First Earl of Lovelace. She brought a team of Swiss mountaineers to Worthy to construct the tunnels, so tradesmen could come and go without their carts being seen from the house. The earl also planted thousands of trees amongst the ancient oaks, including cypress, Canadian and Scots pine, copper beech, bay and cedar, and it's fun trying to spot as many different types as you can once you have walked under what today are known as the Fairy Tunnels. You will also spot other ruins being reclaimed by nature as you continue your walk up through Yearnor Woods.

The landscaped gardens were the stuff of romance and fantasy, consisting of a series of terraces down to the sea with towers, turrets, bridges and follies, all connected by spiral stairs. There were even crenellated battlements curving around the hillside, offering stunning views of the sea. Steps led down to a private beach, where a bath house was constructed to allow Ada to bathe in privacy. Part of the terraces became known as the Philosopher's Walk, as Ada would walk and talk there with the polymath Charles Babbage, with whom she laid out the mathematical principles involved in programming a digital computer. Ashley Combe House was later leased to Dr Barnardo's and used as a nursery in the Second World War, before becoming a doomed Country Club in the 1950s. It fell into disrepair and was sadly demolished in 1974.

The walk climbs and drops as it continues along the wooded pathway, offering occasional tantalising glimpses across the Bristol Channel. Just above Culbone Rocks the walk arrives at the pretty Culbone or St Beuno's Church ❸, which is said to be the smallest (and most secluded) parish church in England. In Simon Jenkins' book, *England's Thousand Best Churches* he describes his arrival at the church "through steep woods of walnut and oak, glorious on a summer's day with the sea glinting through the trees, darkly mysterious and dripping with water in winter."

If the doors to the church are open, it is well worth a visit. Recorded in the Domesday Book, it is believed to be pre-Norman in origin and seats just

30 people. Being so remote, Kitnor (the ancient name for the parish) was known as a place of banishment from 1265 right through to 1751. It was where offenders from the local community were sent for crimes they had committed, before a leper colony was created in 1544. These poor people were also treated as outcasts and given no help of any kind in terms of shelter, food or nursing. They had to create their own shelters, forage for food and cultivate the land as best they could, and are believed to have been the first to work the woods making charcoal. The church still has a 'leper's squint', a tiny window in the north side of the nave that allowed the afflicted to attend church services, standing outside and looking in.

Set in a quiet combe with a beautiful churchyard, this makes a lovely spot for a lunch stop. According to the Porlock Weir website, the hamlet is so hidden that the sun only reaches it for four months of the year. They also record that in 1760, a fair was held in the churchyard "where there was dancing, skittle-playing and much drinking of ale amongst the gravestones" which is a tradition we would very much be in favour of bringing back. The church was used in a television version of *Lorna Doone*, standing in for Oare Church and the heroine's marriage to John Ridd. It also appeared in the video for the Mike and the Mechanics 1988 hit *The Living Years*.

Once spiritually refreshed, you can resume a steep walk up through the oak and sycamore woods of Withy Combe, where you will eventually be rewarded with extraordinary views across to the Gower in Wales. You are following the route that Samuel Taylor Coleridge was walking on the day he dreamed up one of his most famous poems,

Kubla Khan. He was said to be staying at Ash Farm ❻, where he took two grains of opium (which he always claimed was purely medicinal when he was suffering from a headache or upset stomach). In his trance he composed two or three hundred lines of poetry in his head, and when he awoke he started to write it down.

Famously, he was interrupted by a man on business from Porlock (possibly Dr Aaron Potter, who supplied his laudanum), which delayed his writing by about an hour. After this pause he could only remember some eight or ten more lines of the poem. According to Coleridge, in his introduction to the first publication of his poem, "all the rest had passed away like the images on the surface of a stream into which a stone has been cast, but, alas! without the after restoration of the latter!" The phrase a 'person from Porlock' has since become a term to describe interrupted genius; we have had similar problems after drinking a couple of glasses of wine following a swim walk.

The walk loops back along the Coleridge Way, a beautiful route with far-reaching views, which might inspire you to some poetry of your own. Passing farm buildings and holiday properties, the route eventually enters Worthy Wood ❼, avoiding the toll road that doesn't allow walkers or bikes. The path zig-zags down through the atmospheric twisted oaks of the ancient woodland that cloaks the hillside above Porlock Weir, then drops down behind some houses, before passing Porlock Bay Oysters and returning to the start. Here you could reward yourself with another swim, or perhaps a pint in The Ship Inn – known as the Bottom Ship, as there is another Ship Inn in nearby Porlock itself, obviously known at the Top Ship.

DIRECTIONS

1 From the car park, cross the road and take the path to the right of the Ship Inn, signposted 'Culbone Church'. Follow the signed coast path round to the right and uphill. Go through fields and a wood. You reach a road where you turn right following the sign for coast path and Culbone Church. Ignore track to Worthy Combe and stay on the road bearing right.
0.5 miles

2 At the distinctive curved toll building turn right, under the small arch, signed for coast path and Culbone. Follow the path as it passes through a tunnel with a turret and past another tunnel on the left. The path starts to zig-zag up the hill. Keep following it as it ascends and descends through the woods.
1.4 miles

3 You arrive at Culbone Church. After a look round, stand with your back to the church entrance and walk straight ahead to the end of the graveyard, where you'll find a small wooden gate on the left with an inscription to Stephen John Loader. Go through the gate and

turn right following the sign for Silcombe Farm. Ascend through the wood.
0.3 miles

4 Emerge out of the wood at a T-junction. Turn left following the sign for coast path, Silcombe Farm and Lynmouth. Walk uphill along the track and then emerge into fields with great views back to Hurlstone Point.
0.3 miles

5 You reach a lane. Turn left here for Ash Farm (the sign is tiny; do not go straight on to Silcombe). Follow the lane, ignoring a track to the right, and following signs for Parsonage Farm. Pass through Parsonage Farm, with its chocolate-box buildings, and carry on along the lane.
0.8 miles

6 Pass the entrances to Ash Farm and then Yarner Farm, both on the left. Keep going straight, following the sign for Porlock Weir via Worthy Toll Road. Follow the lane as it descends and then hairpins to the left, again following the sign for Porlock Weir via Toll Road.
0.8 miles

7 You reach the start of the toll road. Fork right off the road here, following the sign for Porlockford and Porlock. Ignore the almost immediate left turn for the bridleway and follow the path ahead through the woods for Porlockford.
0.4 miles

8 Turn left off the main path, following the 'Public Bridleway and Porlock Weir' sign. Follow the path downhill; after a short distance you come to a T-junction with a wider track. Turn left along the track, following the bridleway sign with the blue arrows and continue on the track as it then bears right.
0.5 miles

9 Look for a hairpin left-hand turn off the path, signposted 'Bridleway and Porlock Weir'. This turn is easy to miss; make sure you take it, or else the path will take you right away from where you need to be. Descend the narrow path down through the woods. At the road, turn right and then take the next left by the Somerset County sign, which leads you back down to Porlock Weir.
0.5 miles

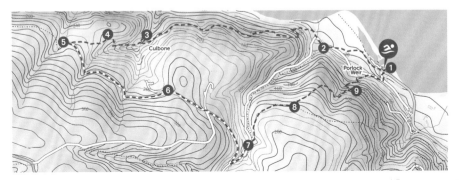

Walk 13

DUNSTER CIRCULAR

The castles, historic villages and breathtaking views of this walk formed the backdrop to the composition of one of the most popular hymns ever. As is common on this part of the coast, you can only swim at high tide, so it's best to start the walk about two hours before high water to arrive at the sea at the optimum time.

oday's walk starts in front of St George's Church ❶ in the charming old market town of Dunster on the northern edge of Exmoor. Cecil Frances Alexander stayed here while writing the hymn *All Things Bright and Beautiful*. The church, which mainly dates back to the 15th century, wasn't always so harmonious. It was once shared between the monks of Dunster Priory and the parishioners, and they didn't always see eye to eye. Eventually a carved rood screen was used to divide the church in half, with each faction taking their own section for worship.

After singing a verse or two, walk away from the church and down the pretty lane, the very epitome of a quintessential English village. You pass the Stags Head, a historic 16th-century inn, which lays claim to being the oldest drinking establishment in the village. As such it's reputedly haunted, and there's also an unlikely legend that it got its name after a wild stag went on a rampage on the premises causing carnage along the way. According to the story, the wild beast was eventually shot and its antlers were hung on the wall as a trophy.

The walk takes you down to the River Anvill, which is supposed to be 'the river running by' from the hymn, with Grabbist Hill as the 'purple headed mountain' above; the 'rich man in his castle' and 'poor man at his gate' are said to reference nearby Dunster Castle. The walk passes over Gallox Bridge ❷, a pretty medieval packhorse bridge that was once the main transport link to carry wool into Dunster for sale.

INFORMATION

DISTANCE: 6.5 miles
TIME: Allow 4 hours
MAP: OS Explorer OL9 Exmoor
START AND END POINT: St George's Church, Dunster (SS 99024 43649, TA24 6SH, What3Words: factoring.thousands.burst)
PUBLIC TRANSPORT: Nearest mainline train station is Taunton, and the 28 bus to Dunster Steep stop takes around 50 mins
SWIMMING: Blue Anchor Bay (ST 01417 43787), but only swimmable at high tide
REFRESHMENTS: There are endless charming places for snacks and refreshments in Dunster, including Locks Victorian Tea Rooms, with gardens for the summer (TA24 6SG, 01643 822001) or The Luttrell Arms Hotel, a remarkable 15th-century hotel with a secret garden that offers amazing views of the castle and deer park (TA24 6SG, 0164 821555)
EASIER ACCESS: There is parking at Dunster Beach and the Steam Coast Trail is very accessible; swimming may be possible to those with limited mobility on a high tide
NEARBY SWIM SPOTS: There's a good community of swimmers at Minehead where you will find people at high tide most days; they meet at steps on the seafront outside Dana's Fish and Chips

The path takes you past a pretty yellow thatched cottage and then onto a bridleway ❸, climbing up onto Gallox Hill ❹. The name derives from the gallows that once stood here; according to the English Heritage, this was "a symbol of authority of the lords of Dunster Castle, who had the right to try and hang any thief caught within the area of their jurisdiction." This was also the site of an Iron Age hillfort, and there is another, bigger one, a little further on at Bat's Castle ❺. which remarkably was identified only in 1983, when some school-boys discovered eight silver-plated coins dating from 102BC to AD350 there. It features two stone ramparts and two ditches, with much of the area now covered in scrub. This is the highest point on the walk, with remarkable views over the Quantock Hills and Exmoor in one direction and over the Bristol Channel to south Wales in the other. It's the perfect place to stop for a snack and a breather.

The walk takes you down the other side of the hill ❻, following paths that become a track and eventually a tarmac lane that leads into the village of Carhampton ❼. There is an Arthurian legend that says that a dragon was terrorising the village, then called Carrum, and that Saint Carantoc tamed or slayed the beast, depending on which version you read. In return, King Arthur gave permission for a monastery to be built, but any evidence of this is long gone.

Today the village is famous for its annual wassailing celebration, started in the 1930s by the Taunton Cider Company, which takes place on 17th January in the community orchard. The villagers form a circle around the largest apple tree and hang pieces of cider-soaked toast in the branches for the robin, who is said the represent the good spirits of the tree. A gun is fired overhead to scare away any evil spirits, and the celebrations continue in the grounds of The Butcher's Arms pub.

After crossing the road, the route continues along Sea Lane and across fields ❽ down towards the Bristol Channel. It then heads up and over the railway tracks of the West Somerset Railway ❾, a 20-mile heritage railway passing through ten stations between Bishops Lydeard and Minehead. It carries 200,000 passengers a year and has featured in many television and films including *The Land Girls*, *The Lion, the Witch and the Wardrobe* and the Beatles classic *A Hard Day's Night*.

It's definitely time for a dip, and if you have timed the walk right and the tide is in, then you can swim here in what is known as Blue Anchor Bay. However, when the tide is out it goes out a long way, so it's all mud and shingle; still an excellent place to look for fossils and part of the Blue Anchor to Lilstock Coast SSSI. On a clear day you can see right across the Bristol Channel to south Wales, while in the other direction you should be able to see Gallox Hill and Dunster Castle, giving you a good idea of the route so far.

It's a lovely walk along South West Coast Path, which is also known as the Steam Coast Trail here. This is part of an ongoing community project to build a network of multi-user paths around west Somerset for walkers, cyclists, runners and mobility scooter and wheelchair users. This is the first of two phases that have opened so far and runs along a 1.3 mile stretch that takes you from near Blue Anchor to Dunster Beach, with its holiday chalets and a seasonal café. The structures behind the car park are Second World War 'pillbox' defences, and you may want to stop and explore the Hawn, a nature reserve behind the beach chalets. It was once part of a medieval port and linked to the channel, but is now a silted-up lake.

The walk then turns inland again, following Sea Lane towards Dunster. It crosses the railway tracks

near Dunster Station, which may look familiar if you ever had a model railway as a child; Hornby produced a popular 1:76 scale model of it, one of which is on display in the station. You then turn onto the Riverside Jubilee Walk footpath ❾.

After crossing the very busy main road ⓫, we continue up through the grounds of Dunster Castle; a dun is an ancient fort, and the village was originally known as Torre. The land was given to the influential de Mohun family to build a castle overlooking the Bristol Channel to protect the coast from invasion. The medieval gatehouse and ruined towers are reminders of the original wooden structure and its turbulent past, while the castle that stands today was built by the Luttrell family as their lavish stately home. They lived there for over 600 years, expanding it several times. Now a Grade I listed building and scheduled monument, it was given to the National Trust in 1976 and opened to the public.

The walk heads back into Dunster itself ⓬ and up the high street. The village is home to over 200 listed buildings, and in the middle of the street you will pass the old Yarn Market, which was once a hub for the Exmoor wool trade. Indeed, such was the importance of the cloth trade in Somerset that there were broadcloths known as Dunsters and Watchets (named after the nearby harbour town). A bell at the top of the Yarn Market would have been rung to announce the start of trading; if you look up today you might spot a hole in one of the roof beams, caused by cannon fire in the Civil War.

As you'd expect from such an ancient village there are lots of annual quirky traditions. On 1st May, the Minehead Hobby Horses visit and dance around the village from the Butter Cross to the castle. On Christmas Eve, the burning of an 'ashen faggot' – a bundle of ash rods – while people sing Dunster Carols takes place at the Luttrell Arms hotel. A more recent tradition is Dunster by Candlelight, which takes place on the first Friday and Saturday in December and sees families and colourful stilt-walkers put up candle lanterns throughout the village in a Lantern Lighting Procession.

1 Start the walk from outside the porch at St. George's Church. Head straight out onto West Street and walk past the Stags Head on the right. Turn left down Mill Lane and then right following the sign for Gallox Bridge onto a public bridleway. Bear left past the car park, past Rose Cottage on the left.
0.3 miles

2 Cross Gallox medieval packhorse bridge and carry straight on, following signs for Bat's Castle. After the thatched cottage on the right you reach a junction of paths. Carry straight on, taking the middle path uphill which is signed for Bat's Castle.
0.4 miles

3 You reach a fork; bear left here continuing up the hill. The route flattens out and then starts to rise again. Bear left and go through the deer gate which is signposted for Gallox Hill and Bat's Castle.
0.4 miles

4 You reach Gallox Castle hillfort. Follow the path across the ridge.
0.4 miles

5 You reach Bats Castle hillfort. Continue to follow the path south-east and start to descend.
0.4 miles

6 Go through the deer gate and turn left, following the sign for Carhampton. Descend on the main track, ignoring any turns off to the left or right. The track becomes a tarmac lane and you enter the village of Carhampton.
1.2 miles

7 Just after Laurel Cottage on the right, turn left into High Street; the community orchard is on your right here. At the T-junction cross the road to the Carhampton Stores and turn right. Turn left at Rose Cottage opposite The Butcher's Arms down Sea Lane, which becomes a track.
0.3 miles

8 You reach two gates. Take the public footpath through the right-hand gate and follow it along the left-hand side of the field. Go through a kissing gate and follow the path through three more fields, aiming for the sea and the railway crossing, which has a red sign.
0.7 miles

9 Cross the railway line onto the beach, where you can have a swim at high tide. After your swim, head west along the path (which is known

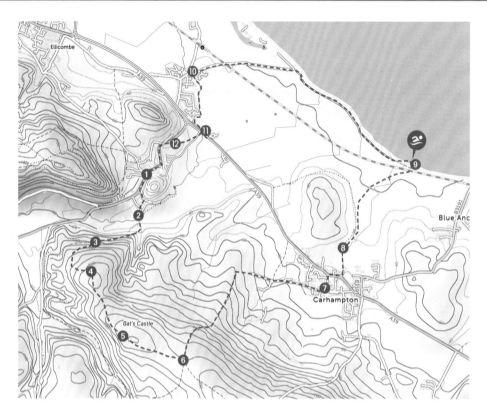

as the Steam Coast Trail for this stretch), with the sea on your right. Cross the flood relief channel and at the car park turn left onto the lane, heading away from the beach and back towards Dunster. (To visit the Hawn, walk on along the shore and then behind the chalets on the left.) Cross the railway line again and pass Haven Close on your left.
1.6 miles

10 Turn left following the sign for Riverside Jubilee Walk to Dunster village, with the river on your right.

Follow the path, ignoring the bridge to the right signed Riverside Jubilee Walk. The path follows the river around the edge of fields, with the main road on your right at the end.
0.4 miles

11 Cross the main road and then take the public footpath immediately on the left, walking into the National Trust Dunster estate. Cross the estate road and follow the path that leads uphill into the trees.
0.2 miles

12 You see the car park on your right. Walk through and turn left onto the main road past the Exmoor National Park Centre on the left. Pass the Yarn Market on your right and then follow the road around right (Church Street) back to the church.
0.3 miles

Walk 14

EAST QUANTOXHEAD AND ST AUDRIE'S BAY

A walk that takes you from picturesque villages to dramatic clifftops with views across the Bristol Channel to Wales. As is usual along this part of the coast, the swims can only be done at high tide, so time your walk accordingly.

INFORMATION

DISTANCE: 6 miles
TIME: Allow 6 hours
MAP: OS Explorer Explorer 140 Quantock Hills & Bridgwater
START AND END POINT: East Quantoxhead Car Park (ST 137 435, TA5 1EJ, What3Words: mirroring. recount.device)
PUBLIC TRANSPORT: The 23B bus between Taunton and Williton runs Monday to Friday and stops in Kilve, about 0.75 miles from the start of the walk
SWIMMING: Kilve Beach (ST 1442 4444), metal steps (ST 1363 4426), St Audrie's Bay (ST 1128 4346) but swimming is only possible at high tide
REFRESHMENTS: Chantry Tea Gardens offers delicious refreshments (try the homemade scotch eggs or cream teas with homemade jam) served by friendly staff in the stunning garden ruins of the ancient chantry (01278 741457, TA5 1EG). The Plough Inn in Holford is a friendly and very affordable pub that has a great beer garden and is dog friendly (01278 741624, TA5 1RY)
EASIER ACCESS: There is a car park very near Kilve Beach that gives access to the grassy area there to take in the views. There is also a shortcut near the start of the route, leading through the fields directly to the set of metal steps
NEARBY SWIM SPOTS: Burnham Beach at Burnham-on-Sea is a great sandy spot to swim before taking a stroll down the shortest pier in the country; alternatively head into the touristy action at Minehead and enjoy a swim from The Strand

Today's walk starts in the pretty little hamlet of East Quantoxhead ❶, with its thatched cottages, medieval tithe barn, duckpond and mill house. You park in the car park of the church, just outside the gate to the estate buildings. The church is dedicated to St Mary and dates to the 14th century, although the estate itself is much older. It was given to the Paganel family just after the Norman conquest and no part of it has been sold since – though in 1207 it passed by marriage to the Luttrell family, who also owned nearby Dunster castle. In the past the village had a small harbour that imported limestone for local limekilns and exported alabaster. The manor house with its medieval tower (called Court House since it served that function in the 19th century) isn't open to the public, but the gardens are from time to time. Do try the local apple juice available from the honesty box – it's delicious.

The walk sets off past the duck pond and takes you across fields, skirting the edge of East Wood ❷. The whole area has the feeling of being lost in time, and long walks in this remarkable landscape inspired William Wordsworth and Samuel Taylor Coleridge as they wrote their landmark *Lyrical Ballads*. After crossing a small ford, you will arrive at the dovecot and the remains of the manor and chantry chapel at Kilve ❸. A chantry was a chapel founded by the rich to pay their way out of purgatory by funding clergy to pray for their souls. This one was set up in 1329 by Simon de Furneaux, and is thought to have been home to five priests.

The buildings fell into ruins even before the dissolution of the monasteries, and for centuries were used as a barn for the nearby farm. They were also used by smugglers, and it is believed that a fire in 1848 was caused by the bootleggers as they were trying to destroy evidence of their contraband brandy. The ruins were placed on the 'at risk' register in 2000, due to the poor condition of the grey shale and Quantock sandstone masonry and the perilous lean on the south gable wall. However, thanks to a grant from Historic England and the support of the owner and volunteers, the site has now been saved for the nation.

After perhaps pausing for a cup of tea and slice of cake in the Chantry Tea Gardens, you walk through the Kilve Beach car park and past an unusual-looking brick building with a rusty chimney on top. This is the Kilve oil retort house ❹ and the only remaining memorial to a scheme to extract shale oil on the Quantock coast long before fracking was invented. In 1922 a Dr William Forbes-Leslie claimed that he could extract and process five million gallons of shale oil a year at Kilve and transport it along a new 11-mile railway to a fuel terminal at Bridgewater docks. He asked speculators to invest £1.5 million (around £68 million in today's currency) promising them that he could double their money in months.

The scheme seemed feasible, as the local shale was known to have special qualities and could be set alight by beach bonfires.

However, it all turned out to be a scam, and the investors lost every single penny. The scandal rocked the financial world, and a judge sent Forbes-Leslie, who he deemed "a highly dangerous and plausible criminal" to jail. And so ended the Somerset oil boom, a lesson it seems the locals took to heart; drilling licences granted in the county in recent years have provoked vigorous protests.

The walk now reaches the coast at Kilve Pill, once a tiny port ❺, and passes along remarkable Kilve beach, known for its fossils and Jurassic geology. The beach is part of Somerset's Jurassic Coast, which runs from Lilstock to Blue Anchor, and its geological importance has seen it being declared an SSSI. On a high tide it is possible to swim here, although our recommended spot is a little further on, and it is also a lot of fun to explore the rocks and rock pools on a low tide. Striking limestone cliffs are layered with glistening white marlstone and oil-rich black shale, while natural slate causeways across the shingle make the beach navigable. It's a fantastic spot for fossil spotting: we found several ammonites, and you can find the fossilised remains of an extinct oyster known as 'devil's toenails.'

Once you've finished exploring, there are some lovely grass banks above the beach for a picnic, with views across the Bristol Channel to south Wales. The islands you may be able to spot off to the right are Steep Holm, with Flat Holm behind it. If you feel like a sing-song, the video for the Brian Adam's song *Everything I Do (I Do It For You)* was filmed on the beach below you – although some of us still haven't recovered from the 16 weeks it spent at number one during the seemingly endless summer of 1991.

The walk continues along the edge of fields on the clifftop coast path, with views around to Minehead in the distance, until you reach a metal staircase ❻ off to the right that leads down to some concrete steps into the sea. This is the best place to swim at high tide. As you walk down the steps, you will be passing down through a colourful series of geological layers in the headland until you reach the pebbly beach, and once at the bottom, the rocks seem to have formed a natural crazy paving causeway to the water's edge. It is certainly one of the more unusual and dramatic swim spots in this part of the Somerset coast.

After a swim, head back up to the coast path and continue up the hill. Look back as you ascend and you will be able to see the rather sinister-looking Hinkley Point nuclear power station. The verdant grassy fields contrast with the dramatic coastline below, and there are views across to Watchet, Minehead and even inland as far as Dunkery Beacon, which is the highest point on Exmoor. The path is overgrown in places and there's a rather annoying dog-leg around a field and small ravine at one point, before it drops down to the shore at St Audrie's Bay **7**.

This is a pebble, sand and shingle beach, which is great for exploring. There are a couple of waterfalls, although we'd recommend staying away from the cliffs, as they look a bit unstable. You will also notice the big yellow warning signs that explain that the beach is liable to flooding

at a high tide, meaning the coast path (which passes along it) sometimes becomes impassable. Again, this is another potential swim spot on a highish tide, although being the Bristol Channel, the waters are muddy-coloured and weedy, and you may come out with what has been dubbed a 'Clevedon Beard'.

The route returns up the steep hill and back along the coast, before turning inland **8** and along the top of several fields. Look out for a burial mound, before the walk heads out of the fields and along a farm track **9** then bears across a field towards the church **10** from the start of the walk. The path then passes some medieval tithe barns and an old engine house and cart shed as it returns to the car park, where some well-earned Somerset apple juice from the honesty box will hopefully still be waiting for you.

DIRECTIONS

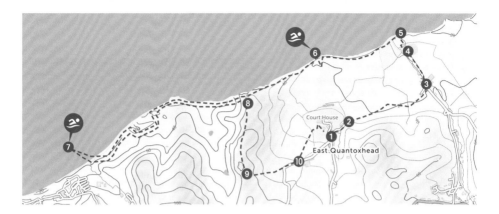

1 From the car park turn right into the lane and then immediately bear left to walk around to the other side of the duck pond. Follow the sign with the yellow arrow signed 'Footpath to beach and Kilve'.
0.2 miles

2 You pass a path on your left signposted to the beach (easier access shortcut to 6). Ignore this and carry straight on, following the sign for Kilve Church. Walk along the right-hand side of the field with the wood on your right. Continue through another field following the 'Quantock Hills' sign, enter a third field and follow the path as it bears to the left. Cross a small ford.
0.6 miles

3 You reach a hamlet with a church on the right and a house and dovecot on the left. Turn left past the ruined chantry chapel and walk through Kilve Beach car park.
0.2 miles

4 At the chimney bear right and follow the track past a ruined building. Then bear left at the fork following a yellow 'Public Footpath' sign.
0.1 miles

5 You reach the coast, and can explore and possibly even swim here on a high tide. To continue, take the coast path heading west, with the sea on your right.
0.5 miles

6 You reach a path to the left, signed for East Quantoxhead (easier access shortcut). Ignore this, and instead immediately look on your right for the staircase down to the beach. This is an ideal swim spot at high tide. Carry on along the coast path, with the sea still on your right. Follow signs saying 'England Coast Path'.
1.8 miles

7 You reach the beach at St Audrie's Bay. This is another potential swim spot on a high tide.

After a dip and exploration of the beach, retrace your steps back along coast path and back up the steep hill.
1.3 miles

8 At the top of the hill turn right, following the sign saying 'East Quantoxhead 1m'. Walk through three fields; you will notice a large burial mound on the right in the last field.
0.4 miles

9 You reach a seven-bar metal gate. Turn left down the track, following the sign with the yellow arrow. Bear left onto the lane.
0.3 miles

10 You reach two gates on your left. Go through the second gate, following the public footpath sign, and walk diagonally across the field towards the church and Court House. On the right before the church is a small gate that will take you past farm buildings and back into the car park.
0.3 miles

Walk 15

EAST LYN ADVENTURE

A walk along both sides of the magical East Lyn
River, with swims in several of its beautiful pools.
Bring water shoes to protect your feet.

INFORMATION

DISTANCE: 5.5 miles
TIME: 5 hours
MAP: OS Explorer Map OL 9 Exmoor
START AND END POINT: Car park
at Brendon Village Hall (SS 765 481,
EX35 6PT, What3Words: dairy.
haircuts.monument)
PUBLIC TRANSPORT: None
SWIMMING: Ashford Pool (SS 753
479), Horner Pool (SS 748 487), Long
Pool (SS 752 483)
REFRESHMENTS: The National Trust
café at Watersmeet is perfectly placed
halfway around the walk and serves
cream teas, soups and snacks (EX35
6NT, 01598 753348); the Rockford Inn
is towards the end of the walk, just
when you might be needing a pint, and
has tables by the river (EX35 6PT,
01598 741214)
EASIER ACCESS: Unfortunately, all the
pools on the walk require you to walk
some distance, and involve a degree of
climbing down rocks to get in. If you
park at Rockford and then cross the
river there is a nice pool about 300
yards downstream to the west (SS 753
479; point 3)
NEARBY SWIM SPOTS: Lee Bay, just
west of Lynton, is a lovely cove;
Badgworthy Water

The East Lyn is a picturesque and romantic river, with
fantastical rock formations, cliffs and islands, giving
it a feel of fairyland. It carves its way through ancient
woodland, forming unusual shapes and the most
atmospheric pools for swimming. The route takes us first downstream, as the river tumbles towards the sea at Lynmouth, and
then back upstream on the other bank, which gives a different
perspective on the first half of the adventure.

The walk starts at Brendon Village Hall ❶, where there's an
honesty box to pay for your parking; at the time of the writing the
suggested donation is £2. There's an information centre housed
in an old stone building, which is well worth a visit. It has maps
and displays about the history, geography, botany and geology
of the area, including some particularly fascinating old photos
of Victorian tourists who came to explore the stunning scenery
and the lush vegetation along the river's banks. In the mid-19th
century, a craze had started for ferns in particular, and in 1856
Charlotte Chanter published a book called *Ferny Combes* which was
an account of travelling all over Devon in search of these exotic-
looking and ancient plants.

Charlotte lived here in Brendon with her husband, clergyman
John Mill Chanter, and her house, Millslade, is now a B&B.
Turning left from the car park, with the river on your left, this
is the first dwelling you pass on your right. The route continues
through this quiet village, past the Staghunters Inn, and then
crosses an old stone bridge before heading west along the East
Lyn River from the other side. Just after crossing the main bridge,
and leaving the main road, look out for a tiny bridge on the left,
with cobblestones ❷. This is an old packhorse bridge, thought

to date back to the 17th century, and the intricacy of the stonework and placement of the cobbles is quite remarkable.

You're now walking on the Coleridge Way, a 50-mile footpath through Somerset and Devon commemorating the life and work of the romantic poet Samuel Taylor Coleridge. It starts at his home at Nether Stowey in the Quantocks and finishes in Lynmouth, so this section is near the end of the trail. You pass through the grounds of Countisbury Mill, which once used the power of the river to grind corn, but which is now a private house. Soon you are alongside the river again, as it rushes downstream through a dramatic gorge. These dark blue-grey slates and sandstones are part of the Lynton Beds, formed around 400 million years ago in the Devonian period, and the water has formed an enchanting sequence of falls and pools here.

The hamlet of Rockford lies on the other side, and you can get across to via a footbridge if you fancy a quick detour to the pub, but we'll be coming back that way later so perhaps hold off for now. You're now in an SSSI; Natural England says it is "one of the largest remaining semi-natural ancient woodlands in south west Britain, with rare and local plant species and rich breeding bird populations" as well as notable geological features. Birds that breed here include redstarts, pied flycatchers, willow warblers and wood warblers; the woods are famed for their rare whitebeam trees, and are home to over 50 species of lichen, as well as rare ferns.

Shortly after passing Rockford the pools in the river get bigger, and you soon reach the first swim spot, Ashford Pool ❸. The river cascades down through a chunky waterfall, which is framed by an ivy-covered cliff behind, creating the feeling of a watery dell. The pool under the cascade is deep

and you can get a good massage by bracing yourself against the bubbles. You can then swim down a channel below the pool into another, wider pool below. The river is full of boulders and crags, and altogether feels prehistoric, like being lost in time.

This river is famed for sea trout and salmon, which anglers are required to return to the river alive. You might encounter people fishing on this side, managed by the National Trust, which allows it; the other bank is all private fishing. There were a couple of anglers there last time we visited, and we all respected each other's pursuits, exchanging stories of our riparian adventures.

The route continues along the river past Ash Bridge ❹ a pretty footbridge. Shortly after you'll find a beach with an island, which is a nice place to stop if you've got small children, as it's ideal for paddling. About 5 to 10 minutes' walk further on is Horner Pool ❺, another lovely swimming spot. It's a short scramble down off the path, but is long and deep, with a moss-covered wall on one side.

The next point of interest is Watersmeet ⑥, where the East Lyn meets Hoar Oak Water. Here you'll find a National Trust tearoom, housed in a rather elegant old Tudor Gothic style building, which was built as a fishing lodge in 1832 by the Reverend Walter Halliday, who had come into a large inheritance, and Historic England says it may originally have been thatched. It has a delightful garden, and is a lovely place to sit and have a breather.

After some refreshment, cross the bridge over the river, from where you can admire a spectacular waterfall. The route then heads back upstream on the path closest to the water, with the river on your left. You soon pass a pair of lime kilns, also built by the Reverend Walter Halliday, to create lime for fertilising fields and making mortar. You pass Ash Bridge again, and then shortly after that, you reach Long Pool ⑧, where there is a small bench.

Long Pool has a very different feel from the previous pools on the walk; it really is an unforgettable spot. It is well over 50 metres long, narrow and dark, with imposing walls either side; it has a slightly melancholy, brooding air. It's a bit like swimming in an elongated tunnel.

After a swim, continue along the path which starts to go uphill and away from the river. It eventually joins the narrow road ⑨ that descends to Rockford. When tourists started visiting in cars and charabancs in the 1920s, this was notorious for both hold-ups and accidents as vehicles tried to squeeze through. An article from the Exeter Gazette of 1926 with the headline "Several Injured" lamented "another accident" in which a car overturned, injuring its occupants, who were treated by the local doctor.

In Rockford, you may well want to stop for a drink in the pub, which has tables overlooking the river. From here you follow the lane all the way back to the village hall where you parked.

1 Turn left out of the car park onto the road and walk with the river on your left. You reach a grassy triangle in the middle of the road. Turn left here, cross the bridge and turn left following sign for Porlock, Lynmouth and Lynton.
0.5 miles

2 When the road starts to bear right uphill, take the track straight ahead, following the sign for Rockford and Watersmeet. The river is on your left. Follow the track through the grounds of Countisbury Mill and join the path by the river. The track starts to ascend and you pass a National Trust sign for Watersmeet. You pass a footbridge to the hamlet of Rockford; do not cross but continue walking with the river on your left, following the sign for Watersmeet, Countisbury and Lynmouth. You will start to notice potential swimming spots in the river!
1.3 miles

3 This is the first swim spot: Ashford Pool, underneath a cliff with a waterfall. After a dip, continue walking with the river on your left.
0.6 miles

4 You reach a footbridge; this is Ash Bridge. Do not cross but continue walking with the river on your left, passing a pretty beach with an island, which is a lovely spot to stop if you have young children who would like a paddle.
0.5 miles

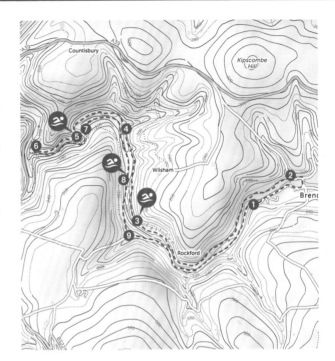

5 You reach Horner Pool, another place to swim. It's a bit of a scramble down but perfectly doable. After, continue walking with the river on your left.
0.3 miles

6 You reach Watersmeet, where you can stop for a break and something reviving. Cross the bridge to the opposite side of the river and turn immediately left. You're now walking back along the other side of the river, with the river on your left, and you pass a lime kiln.
0.4 miles

7 You reach a junction with a sign saying 'Barton Wood'. Bear left here following the sign saying 'Footpath Rockford'. Keep walking with the river on your left, passing Ash Bridge (point 4).
0.6 miles

8 You reach Long Pool, which has a little bench by it; stop here for another swim. After, continue to follow the path as it leads uphill and away from the river. Another path joins from the left.
0.3 miles

9 At the road, turn left and follow it all the way back to the car park.
1 mile

Walk 16

BADGWORTHY WATER
AND DOONE COUNTRY

A stunning if strenuous walk over the moors followed by numerous dips in idyllic Badgworthy Water, famous as the setting for the Victorian novel Lorna Doone. Take wet shoes to protect your feet, as the riverbed is stony.

Today's walk is a tough one with a lot of ascents, but it is full of contrasts, taking in everything from the bleak beauty of the high moor to ancient woodlands and a magical river. If you're not feeling energetic, the swim spots can be reached by walking a simple 'out and back' up the river from the start point to the campsite at Cloud Farm.

However, if you're up for the full experience, the walk starts in the hamlet of Malmsmead ❶, home of Lorna Doone farm but, perhaps more importantly, the site of a very nice National Trust buttery with the added bonus of a wood-burning stove. This tiny settlement is very picturesque, with an ancient ford and a pretty packhorse bridge, both still in use today. The bridge is rather vulnerable because it's so narrow; last time we were here, we found part of a caravan which had been knocked off when a visitor had unwisely decided to drive over it.

Everywhere you go around here you see references to *Lorna Doone*, the eponymous heroine of a novel full of outlaws, adventure and derring-do by RD Blackmore, which was published in 1869. Set in the wilds of 17th-century Exmoor, it tells the story of the villainous Doones and their plan to marry Lorna to the wicked Carver Doone. But she loves John Ridd, a local farmer who rescues her from her fate, and after much drama around Lorna's true parentage and even royal upheaval, they are free to marry. However, on the day of their wedding, a vengeful Carver shoots Lorna through the church window. John pursues him, blazing with rage, and after a struggle, Carver meets an unpleasant end in a bog. Lorna survives and she and John live happily ever after.

INFORMATION

DISTANCE: 8 miles
TIME: Allow all day
MAP: OS Explorer Map OL 9 Exmoor
START AND END POINT: Car park at Malmsmead (SS 791 478, EX35 6NU, What3Words: canoe.cork. pressing)
PUBLIC TRANSPORT: The nearest bus stop is at County Gate car park, served by the Exmoor Coaster bus route. Part of the Coleridge Way follows a field edge 0.6 miles from the car park down into Malmsmead
SWIMMING: Several pools in Badgworthy Water, which we have given names for easy reference. Breakfast pool for its proximity to the campsite (SS 793 467), Memorial pool (SS 793 464), and Deer Park Pool (SS 792 453)
REFRESHMENTS: The National Trust Buttery at Malmsmead serves light lunches and teas (EX35 6NU, 01598 741362); there is also a shop that sells snacks at Cloud Farm campsite
EASIER ACCESS: The pools in Badgworthy Water are most easily accessed from Cloud Farm, where there is a car park. However, you need to ring the campsite to ask permission to park (01598 741190). Once there, it is a gentle walk uphill to the pools, and the nearest is right next to the campsite, but a small amount of scrambling the bank is needed, and the riverbed is stony.
NEARBY SWIM SPOTS: The East Lyn River has some beautiful pools, and there is good swimming at Lynmouth

119

In truth, the novel is now very old-fashioned and it's hard to imagine it finding many new readers today, but it has never been out of print and still has a prominent place in public consciousness, at least in this part of the world. This is probably not just due to its qualities as a novel, but also because it has played a crucial role in publicising this part of Exmoor. Its relentless promotion for tourism purposes started in Victorian times, as soon as the novel started to find success, with even the Ordnance Survey marking the area as 'Doone Country' on the map.

Over the years, fact and fiction have been interwoven, and this is still a topic of debate. There were certainly Doone legends in the early 19th century when Blackmore was growing up here, about a Scottish outlaw family exiled to Exmoor, which must have inspired his story.

The walk starts with a steep climb out of Malmsmead up into Southern Wood ❷, which is full of ferns and elegant twisted oak trees as well as a slightly incongruous group of Scots pines. You emerge onto open moorland ❸, heading over Malmsmead Hill towards Brendon Common. The views are spectacular, and the moor can feel anything from benign to bleak, depending on the weather. SH Burton describes it poetically in his 1969 book Exmoor: "Nothing is static here. The curving contours rise and fall in an illusion of movement, perfected on a sunny day by the cloud shadows skimming over them, driven by the wind that always blows. In stormy weather, the dark mounds of the barrows and the crests of the ridges loom blackly like the gathering waves of an angry sea."

After a stomp across a section of moor, the route crosses a small stream ❺ bordered by a line of beautiful beech trees growing out of an old wall. It continues down to Lankcombe Ford ❻,

another water crossing, before ascending again and then dropping down to an area called Badgworthy Lees. Here is a definite feeling that man has been at work, unlike the previous moorland section, which feels much wilder and more featureless. There are some beautifully constructed stone walls, and then you will see, to your left, a large pile of stones. This is the site of a medieval village ❼, thought to have been abandoned in the early 15th century.

Although it is hard to make out the signs of them, experts at Historic England say there are the remains of about 14 separate buildings here, the biggest having five rooms. There was a chapel and hermitage, and the foundation of the village is recorded in a charter of 1170, when the land was given to the Knights Hospitallers. Before that it was described as 'the land of the hermits of Badgworthy'. The final mention of it is in 1430, by which time it was being abandoned, probably because of the Black Death, although apparently one house was still occupied at the beginning of the 1800s.

When RD Blackmore was writing Lorna Doone in the late 19th century, the remains of the village were presumably more extensive or visible than they are today. He would have wandered past and seen them, and it's generally agreed that this is the site of the 'Doone village', home of the dastardly Doones, as described in the book by narrator John Ridd: "… on either bank were covered houses, built of stone, square and roughly cornered… only one room high they were, and not placed opposite each other but in and out as skittles are… Deep in the quiet valley there, away from noise, and violence, and brawl, save that of the rivulet, any man would have deemed them homes of simple mind and innocence. Yet not a single house stood there but was the home of murder."

The walk continues past the village and then bears left, heading downhill to the river, Badgworthy Water (pronounced Badgery Water). The first swim spot ❽, Deer Park Pool, is to be found shortly after you cross a wooden footbridge, about a mile on from the medieval village. It's probably the best swimming spot on the walk (there are a couple more to come), with a small waterfall you can lie in at the top of the pool, and brown trout swimming below. The eastern side of the pool is bordered by large blocks, which feel man-made, and on the western side there is a little beach. There is also a lovely flat grassy area right by the pool where it's delightful to dry off in the sun.

After a dip, the route continues downhill alongside the river. You come across the RD Blackmore memorial stone ❾, a slate plaque on an enormous rock, which was erected there by the Lorna Doone Centenary Committee in 1969. It contains an inscription praising Blackmore for a novel that "extols to all the world the joys of Exmoor." There is another pool right by the memorial, which is narrow but deep in the middle. There are also benches, very handy for any in the party who do not wish to swim!

The final swim spot on the walk is right by the campsite at Cloud Farm ❿. Before crossing the footbridge, walk back a little way upstream to find it. There isn't really a path, but you can scramble along the bank, where you'll find the remains of the footings of a bridge at the bottom end of the pool. There is a beautiful 'staircase' of cascades above, descending down into the pool, which are particularly special because you can't really see them from the main footpath. Swimming in the centre of this pool, with the water tumbling down above you, is a joy. It can also be accessed from the campsite side.

The walk continues over the footbridge and through the campsite, which is an idyllic position in the valley. It's been visited by tourists for well over a hundred years; the 'Cloud Farm Tea Garden' is mentioned in early guidebooks, and it has long been a camping spot. In 2020, just before lockdown, the National Trust bought the site for £1.5M, and now runs the campsite. At the time, Rob Joules from the Trust described it as "like one of those places that time has forgot. It is remote and very beautiful. You see herons in the winter, deer on the hillside. It's pitch-black at night, just the sound of the river and birdsong."

The campsite has a shop and toilets, which could be useful at this stage of the walk. After a pitstop, the final section of the walk ascends again and then drops down to the hamlet of Oare ⓬. Here you will find the 'Lorna Doone' church, the scene of the wedding day shooting in the book; look for the narrow window in the south wall where, in Blackmore's imagination, the shot came in. There is a memorial plaque to the author, which is a replica of one in Exeter Cathedral, and an extraordinary medieval piscina in the form of a head. The church has rather a sombre feel, with dark box pews and an unusual chancel arch covered with wood from the wagon roof. In the summer, swallows nest in the porch.

The final section of the walk continues along a quiet lane, taking you back to Malmsmead and the welcome sight of the National Trust tearoom.

① From the car park, head towards the National Trust buildings but don't go around to the tea shop. Look for a large corrugated iron barn on the right, and take the track immediately to the right of it, signed Public Bridleway Southern Wood. Follow the track uphill and into the wood.
0.4 miles

② At the top, where it flattens out and starts to descend, you reach a fork. Bear left here and walk downhill to meet a road. Turn left and then immediately left off the road and back into the wood, following the sign for Public Bridleway Brendon Common.
0.4 miles

③ You leave the wood, going through a gate signed Bridleway and Brendon Common. You're now walking on the open moor. Very soon you reach a crossroads of paths where there is a hawthorn tree; go straight ahead here. Then, after another short distance, there is another junction with a small sign with blue arrows indicating a bridleway; bear left

here. Shortly after you reach another fork where you bear left.
0.3 miles

④ You reach a gate onto the road signed Permitted Bridleway, Dry Bridge, Badgworthy Valley. Go through the gate and cross the road continuing straight ahead. After a short distance you reach a fork; bear right here. The route starts to go downhill and you see a group of beech trees growing out of a wall on your right.
0.5 miles

⑤ Cross the stream and bear left at the fork. Follow the path as it veers to the right, away from the stream. You reach a small post with a blue arrow on top; keep following the track here as it bears right.
0.8 miles

⑥ Turn left off the track, following the sign with the blue arrow for Bridleway and Doone Country. Cross the stream and take the path uphill and to the left. Go through a metal gate, following the signed bridleway with the blue arrows. Follow the path as it descends.
1.6 miles

⑦ Pass the site of the medieval village (basically a pile of stones) on your left. Follow the path until you reach a left turn signed for Malmsmead; go left here and keep following signs for Malmsmead. You now have the river on your right, and the path descends until you're walking by the river. Cross a footbridge.
1 mile

⑧ Shortly after the footbridge you will find the first – and best – swim spot. Deer Park Pool is a lovely circular pool with a small waterfall. After a dip, continue walking with the river on your right.
0.7 miles

⑨ You reach the huge stone RD Blackmore memorial, which you can't miss. There are benches, and another swim spot right here by the memorial, smaller than the first but still quite deep. After, continue walking with the river on your right.
0.3 miles

⑩ Cross the footbridge over to the campsite, with another lovely pool and a stunning series of cascades just upstream of it. (It is a little tricky to access from the footpath but possible by walking up the west bank; it is marked by the remains of the foundations of an old bridge.). Cross the campsite, going up steps and passing the shop, Carver Cottage and the toilets on your right. Turn left opposite the toilets, passing farm buildings and following signs for Oare, going through a metal gate with a 'private land keep on track'

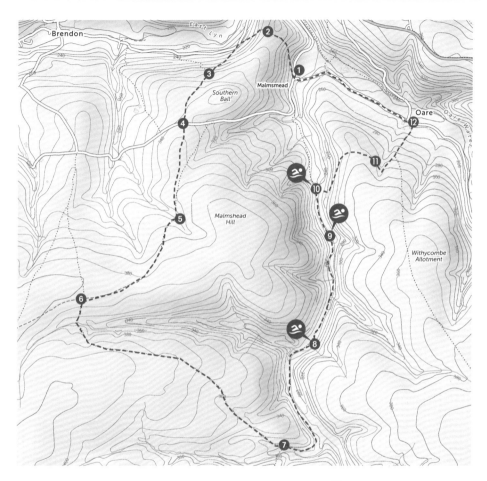

sign. Follow the track uphill, through a wooden gate. It then bears right and flattens out; you go through two fields before the route bears right around the end of the second field.
0.5 miles

⓫ Just after bearing right, turn left through a gateway with a yellow

arrow painted on it, and start walking downhill. The route bears down to the left, signposted Bridleway, Oare. Continue walking straight on downhill following the blue bridleway signs, ignoring the track bending to the right. Follow the signs down to the road where you turn left.
0.4 miles

⓬ You reach the 'Lorna Doone' church on the left. Go in for a look, and if it's summer look out for the birds nesting in the porch. After, follow the road all the way back to the car park.
0.8 miles

HORNER WATER CIRCULAR

A glorious hike onto high moorland followed by a descent into ancient woods and a swim in an enchanting river pool.

INFORMATION

DISTANCE: 6 miles
TIME: Allow 4 hours
MAP: OS Explorer Map OL 9 Exmoor
START AND END POINT: Car park at Horner (SS 897 474, TA24 8HY, What3Words: desks.cycled.signified)
PUBLIC TRANSPORT: None; the Exmoor Coaster and the 10 bus between Minehead and Porlock Weir both stop at Allerford on the A39, about a mile from Horner
SWIMMING: Pool in Horner Water (SS 882 441)
REFRESHMENTS: The Horner Tea Gardens by the car park has the most beautiful flower-filled garden, where you can sit outside, and serves lunches and cream teas (01643 862132, TA24 8HY)
EASIER ACCESS: Unfortunately, the swim spot is deep in the woods and there are no other pools nearer the car park; the river is mostly pretty shallow.
NEARBY SWIM SPOTS: There's a good community of swimmers at Minehead; you will normally find someone to swim with if you visit at high tide. Porlock Weir is stunning at high water

This is a walk of two halves. It starts with a challenging climb up onto Ley Hill, high on Exmoor, where there are breathtaking views over the sea to the north and Dunkery Beacon to the south. The second half is more relaxing: a downhill amble through the magical Horner Valley, with a much easier stroll back to the start.

The walk begins at the National Trust car park at Horner ❶, where you will see a gate to Horner Farm. It's owned by the Trust, and rented out to a young family, who are following regenerative farming practices with the aim of restoring the land and increasing biodiversity. They breed goats, sheep and cattle and have a small shop which is open at the weekends. They also run events including feast evenings, pizza nights and farm tours; it's worth taking a look at their website to see if anything is on when you're visiting (www.horner-farm.co.uk).

From the car park, the route crosses a diminutive late-medieval packhorse bridge. Its surface is cobbled, which you rarely see, and the sides were built deliberately low, to avoid horses' loads being knocked as they crossed. From here, you start to ascend into woods; be prepared for a long, steady climb for the next hour or two of the walk.

Horner Wood is a National Nature Reserve within the Holnicote Estate, which was given to the National Trust in 1944 by Sir Richard Acland. It's thought to be Britain's largest area of ancient woodland and is home to a huge variety of trees as well as rare lichens, ferns, fungi and mosses. The moist atmosphere here means the wood is generally considered to be a temperate rainforest. Sadly, at the time of writing, it has been affected by ash dieback, so you may find some paths are closed because of felling work.

The route, signed for Ley Hill ❷, ascends through Halse Combe, where a tiny stream trickles downhill to your left. One of the unusual features of this area is the length of the woodland edge running beside the moorland, which extends for nearly 10 miles. This is a valuable habitat for insects because it provides a sheltered, warm environment; the rare heath fritillary and green hairstreak butterflies are to be found here.

Eventually you emerge out onto the open moor and start to get the most wonderful views over to the north-east, where you can see the magnificent hog's-back cliffs at Hurlstone Point, the Bristol Channel and over to Wales. For a short distance you walk along a path called Granny's Ride; it's thought to be named after a member of the Acland family, but nobody really knows. You then pass an enormous stone bench, known as Pentley Seat ❺, a memorial to Charles Acland and his wife Gertrude, which is ideally placed for you to stop and have a breather before continuing the climb.

The route continues up Ley Hill, and onto Flora's Ride ❻, another track named after a member of the ubiquitous Acland family. Centuries ago this area was crossed by several packhorse routes: pity the poor ponies who would have had to walk the same route as you have just done, bearing heavy loads of oak bark and other products. Eventually the track flattens out, and you have amazing views ahead of Dunkery Hill and Dunkery Beacon, the highest place in Somerset. It was used as a fire signal station from the 14th to the mid-17th centuries, because of its visibility for miles around; the flames burning on the top of the hill would certainly have been a most magnificent sight.

Flora's Ride eventually starts to descend, and you take a path off it ❼ leading away from the moor and back into the woods, where you will be greeted by the enchanting sight of thousands of spindly sessile oak trees. It feels like a scene from *A Midsummer Night's Dream*. Unusually, there are clouds of mauve heather covering the forest floor: combined with the silvery lichen that clothes the trees, this creates a rather ethereal atmosphere, especially when the sunlight dances through the branches. The path eventually reaches Horner Water, which flows all the way through the woods and then out to the sea at Bossington.

It is a charming little river with many cascades and pools, but only one that is big enough for swimming. The pool ❾ is to be found about 3 minutes' walk after you join the river, and is just above a footbridge. The best access is from the other side, so cross the footbridge and from here you can get in easily. There is a lovely tiered waterfall with wide rock ledges where you can sit and enjoy the flow of the water; the pool itself is fairly small but is a beautiful place for a plunge. Persons unknown have increased the depth by making a dam of large stones.

After a swim, you cross back over the footbridge, turn right and simply follow the river back to Horner, a distance of about 3 miles. This is a wonderfully relaxing walk: it is completely flat, and you can choose to follow lots of little paths that cling to the river bank, or else just stick to the main track if you prefer. It's hard to believe there are no more swimming spots along this stretch, as you keep getting glimpses of promising pools, but unfortunately there is nothing very deep. However, you pass several islands and also little beachy areas, which are perfect if you have paddlers in the party, particularly small children.

The wood feels wild and magical, but for centuries it was a working environment. An estate

survey from 1809 shows the wood was divided into tenements, with local people renting different areas; evidence of boundary banks can be found throughout the wood, particularly near the valley bottom. Wood from the trees was used for fencing, fuel, and to make handles for tools. Charcoal was produced here, and the bark of the sessile oak trees was used in the tanning industry. Tanning in Somerset dates back to the medieval period, and there are references to bark being exported from Horner as far back as 1572. The bark of the little oak trees continued to be harvested right up until the mid-20th century.

Last time we visited, the wood was quite badly affected by ash dieback, and you may come across signs explaining that certain paths have had to be closed because of it. Unfortunately, this fungal disease is present in much of the woodland in this area, with many veteran ash trees affected. It spreads quickly, causing the crown of the tree to become brittle and die, and often resulting in the death of the entire tree. The Trust is managing it by cutting down trees that present a danger to the public, but trying to keep as many as possible, partly to see which prove resistant to disease, and also to keep providing a habit for wildlife, including inspects, woodpeckers and bats, for as long as possible. It's also planting new trees.

The walk finishes with the welcome sight of the Horner Tea Gardens, a pretty sandstone cottage surrounded by flowers. It's only open in the summer months, when its beautiful garden full of colour provides a lovely backdrop, given a festive atmosphere by bunting strung between the trees and colourful parasols; all in all, the perfect end to today's walk.

1 Walk out of the car park the way you drove in. At the road, turn left and then immediately right along a narrow path which at the time of writing has a broken and not very visible sign saying 'Public Bridleway and Porlock'. Cross a cobbled packhorse bridge and follow the path as it bears right and heads uphill. Pass a campsite on the righto through a wooden five-bar gate.
0.4 miles

2 Just after the wooden gate, ignore two2 minor paths to the left, cross the stream (which was empty dry) and then turn left following the sign for Ley Hill. Pass under some tall pine trees. The path starts to ascend and becomes quite steep.
0.4 miles

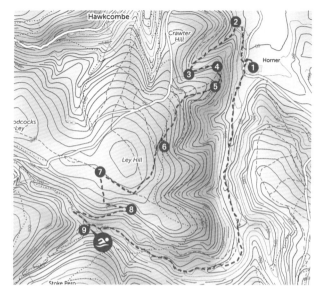

3 You reach a T-junction of paths. Turn left and follow the path as it dips downhill and crosses a stream and then bears left. Start ascending into open moor, with great views down to the left.
0.2 miles

4 At a junction with a small fingerpost keep straight on, following the sign for Granny's Ride. Very shortly you will reach a fork in the paths;, bear right here, going uphill.
0.1 miles

5 Stop for a well-earned breather at Pentley Seat, a huge stone bench on the right,. Stop for a well-earned breather before continuing uphill. You reach a cross-roads of paths; go straight on.
0.5 miles

5 At a T junction where the path meets a track turn right and then almost immediately left (walk for about 40 metres) by a hawthorn tree. Follow the track as it continues uphill. You are now on Flora's Ride. Eventually it flattens out and then starts to descend, and then turns right.
0.7 miles

6 Turn left down a path that switches back from the main track and then enters the woods. Follow the path down through the woods.
0.4 miles

7 You reach a staggered crossroads of paths. Turn right here, continuing to walk downhill until you reach the river. Turn left and follow it downstream for about 3 minutes.
0.5 miles

8 You will find the swim spot just above a footbridge. It's easier to access from the opposite bank, so cross the bridge to get to it and then return back and carry on walking with the river on your right. From here it is a straight, flat walk all the way back, following signs for Horner and passing several footbridges on your right. At various points you can choose to walk along smaller paths by the river, or stick to the main track. Eventually you arrive at a wooden gate marking the entrance to the woods. Go through it and bear right over a bridge, then follow the road back to the tea room and car park.
3 miles

PINKERY POND CIRCULAR

A walk into the wilds of Exmoor that takes you to a legendary swimming spot in the rugged heart of the moor, with a subterranean tunnel if you're feeling adventurous. Bring water shoes to protect your feet.

INFORMATION

DISTANCE: 4 miles
TIME: Allow 3 hours
MAP: OS Explorer OL9 Exmoor
START AND END POINT: Goat Hill car park (SS 725 404, TA24 7LL, What3Words: suffix.personal.thrillers)
PUBLIC TRANSPORT: None
SWIMMING: Pinkery Pond (SS 722 422)
REFRESHMENTS: The nearest is the Black Venus in Challacombe, a dog-friendly traditional pub that serves a good range of food including soups, pies and steaks (01598 763251, EX31 4TT). Withypool Tearooms are by a stone bridge that spans the River Barle and serve soups, savouries and the famous 'Withybig Cream Tea' (01643 831279, TA24 7QP)
EASIER ACCESS: Unfortunately, this is a fairly wild walk with no easy access to the pond itself.
NEARBY SWIM SPOTS: Tarr Steps (20 mins upstream). Woody Bay near Lynton is a great secluded spot that takes a little effort to reach

Today's walk starts at Goat Hill Bridge car park ❶ and leads up onto to a remote and lonely stretch of Exmoor, where a truly isolated and remarkable swim spot is waiting. A good pair of waterproof walking shoes is recommended, as the footpaths often give way to squelchy sections of heather and gorse. It's also a good idea to bring wetsuit boots to protect your feet on the swim. From Goat Hill Bridge ❷ the path heads up towards the utilitarian-looking Pinkery Centre for Outdoor Learning ❸, which has been hosting young people on moorland adventures since 1969. Owned and run by the Exmoor National Park Authority, its aim is to ensure that every new generation is inspired by the landscape and atmosphere of Exmoor.

At the education centre the track changes from tarmac and you follow a winding path that slices its way through the moorland valley just above the stream. Keep an eye out for the stonechats and buzzards who call this bleak section of moorland home. You are now in what was a royal forest in the Saxon period, legally reserved as a hunting ground for the king. In the 13th and 14th centuries the land was deforested, and when Parliament decided to sell Exmoor Forest in 1651 it was described as "mountainous and cold ground, much beclouded with thick fogges and mists and… overgrown with heath and yielding but a poor kind of turf of little value there."

Eventually you arrive at the dam for Pinkery Pond, where a small waterfall splashes out over mossy rocks from a tunnel cut in the rocks below the path ❹. This is actually an overflow for the pond that helps regulate water levels. If you are feeling brave

and the water levels are looking quite sensible, you can walk through the subterranean channel. We changed into swim gear and wetsuit boots and entered the tunnel with some trepidation. It takes a couple of minutes to walk through, and you will need to duck (a head torch would be a good idea) but you will get the most amazing first view of the pond through the mossy exit.

Pinkworthy Pond (pronounced and usually now spelled Pinkery) is an artificial lake that was formed when the headwaters of the River Barle were dammed sometime in the early 1830s. The reservoir and its associated canal were constructed for local landowner John Knight using around 200 Irish labourers, although its purpose has been lost in the sands of time. There are various theories, including that it was to irrigate a stretch of land from Pinkery Farm to Honeymead, or to power agricultural machinery on his new farms or work an incline on a never-completed railway line between Porlock Weir and Simonsbath. It could even be that John Knight just wanted to have a lake on his estate.

Whatever the reasons for its construction, the 170-metre by 100-metre pool makes a fantastic swim spot, tinted a dark Guinness brown. Author Henry Williamson loved to swim here while enjoying a walk from the Chains (which we will come to later), and it even featured in his most famous book, Tarka the Otter. Tarka means 'little water wanderer' and is the name of Sophie's dog, but when we visited on a somewhat blustery spring morning, our Tarka was content to watch us in the water from her sensible position on the sloping banks of the pool.

The peat-based lake is a magical place for a dip, with the refreshing velvety waters making your skin feel wonderful. It's about as wild as swimming can get, and it's blissful gently floating around in circles taking in the rugged moorland that surround you. It's also a popular place to get a 'proper swim' and people do use it to train for events. Those who fancy a bit of extreme fun can sign up for the Man vs Moor challenge; this takes place every June and sees participants dashing across the brutal local terrain, clambering over natural obstacles, making their way through the tunnel and then swimming across the pond in their running kit. It makes us exhausted just thinking about it.

The walk continues on a small spur away from Pinkery Pond and up to Wood Barrow ❺, across what can often be fairly damp and marshy terrain – but reaching some 480 metres above sea level, you will be rewarded with spectacular views. On a clear day you can see Lynmouth Bay to the north and the Bristol Channel in the distance, with views out across Exmoor all around you. Wood Barrow itself is a Bronze Age bowl barrow that was used as a boundary marker for Exmoor Forest, and if you were to follow the path in the direction of the sea, you would pass the Saddle Stone, another forest boundary marker and also one of the original Devon-Somerset boundary stones.

Walking back down the hill towards Pinkery Pond, look out for the yellow, star-like bog asphodel flowers, which add colour to the peat bogs and damp heaths during the summer months before bearing fruit and turning deep orange in the autumn. The Latin name of for the species, *ossifragum*, translates as 'bone-breaker.' This rather threatening name came about because it was once believed that livestock that grazed on it developed brittle bones; it is now understood that the calcium-poor soil of the pastures where it tends to grow caused the problem.

Once back at the pool ❻ we follow the Tarka Trail up to an area known as the Chains, a triangular plateau of Exmoor between Simonsbath, Challacombe and Lynton. The walk takes us up toward the highest point at Chains Barrow, following the bridleway. The area is also the birthplace of several rivers, including the Exe, Barle and West Lyn, and can become a quagmire in the winter months. Even in summer the water levels here led to a tragedy when an estimated 90 million tons of rain fell on north Devon and west Somerset on the 15th of August 1952. An already-saturated area of the moor was unable to absorb all of this additional water, so the rainfall flooded the tributaries of the East and West Lyn Rivers, carrying many tons of soil, boulders and vegetation down through the narrow river valleys. Bridges collapsed and a wall of water and rubble hit Lynmouth in the late evening, leading to a loss of 34 lives. There is a permanent free exhibition at the Flood Memorial Hall in Lynmouth that includes photos, a scale model of the village pre-flood and personal accounts. The exhibition also looks at a recent conspiracy theory that cloud-seeding experiments by the military caused the heavy rainfall.

The walk now turns off down through a post-medieval field drainage system and back down Short Combe ❽ towards the outdoor learning centre. We spotted lots of tadpoles in small pools as we made our way back to the outdoor centre and on to the car park, and apparently, dragonflies are also a common sight both here and up at Pinkery Pond in summer. Incidentally, the Goat Hill car park is listed as an amazing star-gazing site right in the heart of the Europe's first Dark Sky Reserve. So, if you get you timing slightly off and arrive back a little late, don't forget to look up!

❶ From the car park, facing the road, turn right and walk along the road in a north-westerly direction.
0.1 miles

❷ At Goat Hill Bridge, turn right off the main road by the sign for the Pinkery Centre for Outdoor Learning, and following the sign saying 'Access to Pinkery Pond via footpath'. Follow the lane uphill with the stream on your left.
0.4 miles

❸ Bear left opposite the Outdoor Centre following the sign for Pinkery Pond via permissive path. Follow the path as it bears right uphill past a solitary wind turbine. Go through a gate and keep following the path with the stream on your left.
0.7 miles

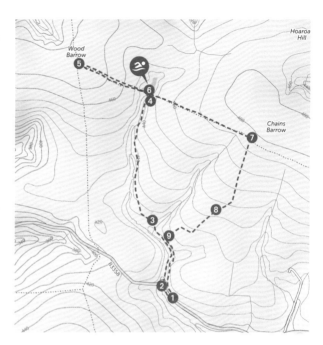

❹ You arrive at a bank with a fence on top; this is the dam for Pinkery Pond. Before ascending to cross to get to the pond, look for the tunnel to the left of the path. At this point you can get changed into water shoes and swim gear and walk through the tunnel to the pond. Alternatively, follow the path uphill to the right, go through the gate at the top and walk down to Pinkery Pond on the other side. After a swim, walk back up to the dam and turn right. Go through a gate and follow the path north-west.
0.5 miles

❺ You reach a junction of paths with a gate, signposted 'Saddle Gate'. Go through to Wood

Barrow on the left, and enjoy the far-reaching views. Then retrace your steps back to Pinkery Pond.
0.5 miles

❻ Pass Pinkery Pond on the left. Carry on walking on the same path in a south-easterly direction, with the fence on your right. You reach a set of two gates on the right; go through the second gate, signposted 'Permitted Bridleway Exe Head'. Continue along the path, with the fence now on your left.
0.6 miles

❼ Turn right, following the sign saying 'Bridleway B3358'. (Chains Barrow with its trig pillar is visible

ahead on the left.) Follow the path downhill, passing a post painted blue on top.
0.5 miles

❽ Go through a five-bar wooden gate and continue to follow the path. Go through a gate for the Pinkery Outdoor Centre and walk down the right-hand side of the field, with the fence on your right.
0.4 miles

❾ You arrive back at the lane you originally walked up. Turn left here and walk back to the car park the way you came.
0.4 miles

LANDACRE BRIDGE FIGURE OF EIGHT

An enchanting walk through the wild Barle
Valley, taking in an Iron Age fort as well as two
freshwater swims; part of the walk involves
fording a river, so make sure you take water
shoes with you.

The walk starts at Landacre (pronounced 'lannacker')
Bridge ❶, a handsome structure with five arches which
dates back to medieval times. It has been an important
crossing place for centuries, linking the northern moor
to an ancient ridgeway track which runs from south-east to north-
west along the crest of Withypool Common. The bridge features
in RD Blackmore's famous novel of Exmoor *Lorna Doone*, where it
is at the centre of a dramatic winter scene: "…the Kensford Water
and the River Barle were pouring down in mighty floods from the
melting of the snow. So great indeed was the torrent, after they
united, that only the parapets of the bridge could be seen above
the water, the road across either bank being covered and very deep
on the hither side." This is rather hard to imagine, given that the
river here is very shallow and only really good for paddling, but it
does make a good story.

The bridge also inspired a dance by the Exmoor Border
Morris. Unlike many Morris sides, which have long and illustri-
ous histories, this group was only founded in 1998, and disbanded
23 years later. However, during those years they were very active
and created many new dances inspired by their love of Exmoor
places and stories, including Porlock Hill, Lorna Doone and Tarr
Steps. You can find them in their bright blue feathery 'tatters' on
YouTube, dancing by the river in 2016.

The first part of the walk takes you up the lane to the north-east
of Landacre Bridge. It's a steep hike, but at least you're getting the
main hill out of the way at the beginning of the walk. Last time
we did this a friendly local who was driving past offered us a lift

INFORMATION

DISTANCE: 6 miles
TIME: Allow 4 hours
MAP: OS Explorer OL9 Exmoor
START AND END POINT: car park
at Landacre Bridge (SS 816 361,
TA24 7SD, What3Words: ashes.
nitrogen.fussy)
PUBLIC TRANSPORT: None
SWIMMING: Pool at Cow Castle (SS
793 374), dipping pool at Sherdon
Hutch (SS 805 360), paddling at
Landacre Bridge (SS 816 361)
REFRESHMENTS: None on the walk,
so take supplies. The nearby
Withypool Tea Rooms is known for its
home-made pasties and sausage rolls
(01643 831279, TA24 7QP). The
Exmoor Forest Inn in Simonsbath
serves meat from its own organic farm
(01643 831341, TA24 7SH)
EASIER ACCESS: Unfortunately the
main swimming spot does involve a
walk; the water is roughly waist deep
at Landacre Bridge, where you start, so
it is good for a tiny plunge but not
really for swimming
NEARBY SWIM SPOTS: Tarr Steps;
Porlock Weir on the coast, at high tide

WALK 19 LANDACRE BRIDGE FIGURE OF EIGHT

to the top; you might be in luck too! At the top of the hill, you turn left off the lane ❷ and head along the Two Moors Way. This is a walking route of 102 miles that links the north and south Devon coasts via Exmoor and Dartmoor, and is marked by blue arrows on the signposts.

As you stride out along the ridge, the initial impression is of quite an empty and even bleak landscape. However, 80 years ago it was a hive of activity, as this area was used for military training. During the Second World War it was used by troops from infantry regiments who dug trenches to store ammunition, and created mounds for field guns. Although you can't really see these features today (they are still visible from the air) they are protected as part of Exmoor's Historic Environment.

The route soon starts to descend, and the Barle Valley spreads out before you in all its glory. The soft curves of the hills, with the river winding through at the bottom, make it one of the most beautiful riverside stretches on Exmoor. The whole valley is an SSSI, protected because of its ancient woodlands, acid grasslands, rare lichens, outstanding birdlife and rare butterflies. If you're lucky you might see red deer, for which Exmoor is famous. There are also, of course, Exmoor ponies roaming, and otters and kingfishers are to be found near the water. Plants in the valley include the bog pimpernel, bog cotton, cow wheat and the insect-eating sundew.

As you reach the river, you enter what used to be the Exmoor Royal Forest. Exmoor became part of the property of the Crown after the Norman conquest. In this context, 'forest' means not an area of trees but an area reserved for hunting by the monarchy and the aristocracy; all deer were the property of the king. Interestingly, Landacre Bridge, where we started the walk, was the meeting place of the Forest Court, which dealt with crimes against the Royal Forest, such as entering with a gun, bow or dog. Over the centuries the Crown's grip loosened and local powerful families took over; the last area of royal forest was sold in 1819.

The route continues with the River Barle on your left (although unfortunately it is fenced off at this point). The river rises on the north west plateau of Exmoor in an area called The Chains. Unusually, its headwaters are now hidden in the expanse of Pinkery Pond, a large lake. Victorian landowners used the river's headwaters to create the lake in around 1830. You pass a footbridge on your left, before crossing a clam bridge over a little stream called the White Water.

This quiet backwater was once the home of one of Exmoor's most famous murderers, William Burgess, who lived there in a now-vanished cottage by the stream in the 1850s. A widower, he killed his six-year-old daughter Anna Maria and hid her body in a flooded copper mine further up the river before fleeing to Wales. The public reports of the trial said he was a hard drinker who resented having to pay for his daughter's upkeep in a foster home. He was hanged at Taunton in 1859, and the case caused enormous shock in the community at the time. Anna Maria was buried in an unmarked grave in St Luke's church in Simonsbath; many years later the Exmoor Society erected a headstone in her memory, which is still there today.

Once across the White Water, you start to see a distinctive hill, ahead and to the right; this is Cow Castle ❺ and just before it is a smaller hill called, suitably, the Calf. Between two and three millennia ago our Iron Age ancestors built a settlement here. It really is the most perfect position, towering above a bend in the river: they could see their enemies coming and there was water nearby.

Not much is known about how they lived, as there is no documentary evidence, but it is thought there would have been a circular wooden palisade around the top of the fort, protecting thatched buildings inside. The fort was protected with a rampart.

It's a steep climb up to the top of the Castle, but the views are superb, and it's a fine place to sit and have lunch, thinking about the people who lived here thousands of years ago. The ribbon of the River Barle snakes into the distance, with the stark hillsides dropping down either side of it.

The first swim spot ❻ is right below Cow Castle, but invisible from the top of the fort. To find it, scramble down the northern side of the hill to the river, where you will see a pool in a very pretty setting, with a wooden fence (to trap debris) across the upstream end. These fences are peculiar

to Exmoor. It is a gorgeous spot, on a bend, tucked under the hill, with a grassy area next to it.

The route continues around the front of the fort to rejoin the path you came along earlier, with the river now on your right. You retrace your steps until the path swings away from the water, then turn right off the main path ❼ and descend down to the river which you will have to ford at this point. Once across, turn right with the river on your right, and in a very short distance you will find a pool ❽ at the point where a stream, Sherdon Water, joins the Barle. This area is known as Sherdon Hutch and has long been a popular spot with local families for paddling and dipping. It is not as deep as the first pool but is very pretty. After your dip, you have a short climb up to a track, which takes you back to the road and thence to Landacre Bridge.

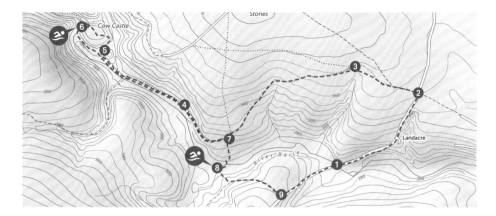

1 From Landacre Bridge, walk up the lane to the north-east, heading uphill.
0.7 miles

2 At the top of the hill, just before a parking area on the right, turn left onto the Two Moors Way, signposted Simonsbath and Thornmead. Walk alongside a beech hedge on your left (ignore a turning off to the right signed 'Byway Thornmead'). At the end of the beech hedge bear right.
0.4 miles

3 You reach a fork. Bear left following the sign for Simonsbath via Cow Castle. The path starts to descend gradually, and you will see the river down below you to the left. At the bottom of the hill, go through a wooden five-bar gate and carry on following the sign for Simonsbath.
1.3 miles

4 You reach a gate by a large beech tree. Go through and carry on with the river on your left. You pass a wooden footbridge over the river to your left (do not cross it, stay on the same side). Shortly after, cross a stream via a clam bridge, still following signs for Simonsbath.
0.6 miles

5 As you see Cow Castle ahead of you, follow the path as it bears around to the right. Shortly after, turn left at the south-east corner of the hill, and climb up it to the top following a rough path. At the top, take in the views before heading down to the other side, again following a rough path.
0.3 miles

6 At the river, immediately under Cow Castle, you will find a large pool where you can stop for a swim. After, follow a rough path at the southern end of the pool with the river on your right. The path tracks around the bottom of Cow Castle until you find yourself again at point 5, having walked a loop around the Castle. Retrace your steps along the river.
1.2 miles

7 Just after the wooden five-bar gate turn right and take the path directly south down to the river. Ford the river and turn right; if you do not wish to ford the river, continue back on the way you came, until you get back to the start.
0.2 miles

8 Shortly after you will reach a large pool where Sherdon Water joins the Barle. This is another place you can have a dip, though it is not very deep. After your swim, if you stand with your back to the river, you will see a rough path going uphill. Take this and follow it as it joins a rough track heading uphill to the east.
0.4 miles

9 Turn left onto the road and follow it back down to Landacre Bridge.
0.4 miles

Walk 20

TARR STEPS AND THE RIVER BARLE CIRCULAR

This is a lovely riverside stroll along the River Barle, with several swimming spots along the tree-lined banks. The route does involve fording the river, which may not be possible if it is in spate, so we have provided alternatives.

oday's outing starts with a walk down the hill from the car park to the River Barle and the legendary Tarr Steps ➋. The 17-span 'clapper bridge' is the longest of its kind in the UK. It marks an ancient fording point, with the steps probably built in the medieval period, although there are some theories that it is much older, possibly prehistoric. The name is from the settlement of Tarr (or Torr) that once existed on the north side of the river, although again there is another theory, that the name comes from *tóchar*, the Celtic word for causeway.

A watermill once stood nearby, and the steps may have been created to help people cross the river to reach it. Some of the stones weigh 2 tonnes, but that doesn't stop them being washed out of place every few years following storms and heavy rains. The bridge has been rebuilt many times, and all the stones are now discreetly numbered so they can be returned to their correct place.

Keep an eye out for the devil, who is said to like sunbathing on the steps. According to legend, the devil built the bridge and threatened to kill anyone who wanted to cross his 'sunbed.' The local villagers did not dare cross and first sent across a cat, who was never seen again – a folk story common across Europe. To solve the impasse, the local parson bravely confronted the devil in the middle of the bridge and forced him to withdraw his threat. Villagers were now allowed to cross, but only if the devil wasn't sunbathing there, a unique Exmoor twist on the tale.

We won't risk crossing the bridge yet, instead taking the path towards Withypool with the water on your left. The River Barle and the surrounding valley are an SSSI. Both the Barle and the Exe

begin their journey up on Exmoor before meeting south of Dulverton and flowing through Devon to reach the English Channel at Exmouth. Fish that may be spotted in the river include salmon, brown trout and bulkhead, while avian visitors include wagtails and the chunky-shaped little dippers. If you are really fortunate, you may even spot the bright blue and orange of a kingfisher diving, or perhaps even an otter.

The river is particularly unpolluted, and the cool oxygenated water flowing over clean gravel creates exactly the conditions needed for salmon to spawn. Atlantic salmon spend time developing into young adult fish before migrating out to sea, where they spend most of their adult lives feeding and growing. Some may journey as far away as Greenland before returning to the same spot where they hatched to spawn. If you're thinking of swimming in the autumn or winter, take care not

to step in the gravelly areas of the river, as this is where the fish lay their eggs. Instead, stand on solid rock to enter the water.

Early in the walk your will pass some steel cables across the river, which are designed to catch fallen trees during flood conditions and protect Tarr Steps below. You will also pass some curious fallen 'money trees,' with hundreds of coins that have been hammered into the branches. The theory is that each coin that you add grants you a wish, a bit like throwing a coin in a fountain or a wishing well. Some wishing trees date back centuries, with an old wives' tale stating that an illness could be cured by transferring it to the tree via the coin.

After about 10 minutes' walk, you'll pass a beachy area ❸ where it is possible to paddle and which would be fun with small children. The route continues under a cloak of oak, silver birch, ash, beech and sycamore trees and over ancient slabs of granite as the river flows by. Lichens, liverworts and mosses thrive in the woodlands, while if you visit in spring, you can expect to see carpets of bluebells and smell wild garlic. Dormice find homes amongst the mature hazel, blackberry and honeysuckle, and several species of bats roost here. It's really not surprising to discover that the area has been designated a National Nature Reserve.

A little further on you enter Hinds Pitt meadow, at the end of which you will find the main swimming spot ❹. It's a lovely big pool, but is better entered from the other side, a little later on in the walk. The route stays on the same side of the river for now, passing a bridge, and you soon reach another place it's possible to swim ❺, although it's not as deep as the main pool. It's just after a small stream, by an open area with a signpost with two yellow arrows. There's a small scramble to reach the river, but it's a lovely verdant spot for a shallow-

ish dip amongst the greens of the trees and plant life lining the river. As the walk continues things start to feel somewhat Tolkienesque, with twisted, moss-covered tree roots to cross over.

You'll then need to cross the river at the ford ❻ towards the beachy area on the other side, where there is a distinctive stand of beech trees. At the time of writing, there is an appeal underway to install a bridge here to safely reroute walkers and horse riders, and to help protect a sensitive area for wildlife and biodiversity. The bridge – which will be known as Great Bradley Bridge – may be in place by the time you visit, but otherwise you will need to take a bit of a paddle (or you could return to the footbridge you passed earlier and cross there).

After fording the river, you turn left and continue back along the other bank. The route passes through open meadows and climbs to higher ground before returning to the river. Just after the footbridge, you will come to the main swim spot ❹ that you saw earlier from the other side, which

is known to locals as Corner Pool. It's a lovely large pool with mossy rocks to put your clothes on and then slabs to step down into the water from under the canopy of trees. There's also a rope swing, which as usual seems to be in a completely inappropriate place and definitely should be avoided. It's a picturesque spot to swim and worth bringing your goggles to look out for fish darting through the clear waters below you.

It's about a 20-minute walk back to Tarr Steps, and you will spot another dipping opportunity along the way ❽, where the path rejoins the river. It's then back to the bridge, where you will finally have to risk the wrath of the sunbathing devil before you cross. Rather conveniently, on your way back to the car park you will pass the Tarr Farm Inn, which has got to be worth checking out. Dating back to the 17th century, this hunting-lodge-style inn has won loads of awards and is a great place for some refreshments; it will definitely help recharge your batteries for the walk back up the hill.

1 From the car park, walk downhill past the toilets on your right and pick up the path that runs beside the road down to Tarr Farm Inn and then Tarr Steps.
0.4 miles

2 At Tarr Steps, do not cross, but turn right, following the yellow arrow saying 'Permitted Footpath Withypool'. You're now walking with the river on your left. You pass a metal structure across the river designed to trap debris.
0.2 miles

3 You reach a beachy area which is a nice place to stop if you've got small children who'd like to paddle. Carry on walking with the river on your left. Cross a stream where there is an old wooden clam bridge to the right, and follow the yellow arrow signed Withypool through Hinds Pitt meadow.
0.6 miles

4 At the end of the meadow, you will find the main swimming spot on a bend. You can go in here, or from the other side later on in the walk. There is another potential swim spot coming up on this side so you may prefer to wait. Carry on walking with the river on your left, passing a wooden footbridge.
0.7 miles

5 You reach an open area with a signpost in the middle with yellow arrows, where there is another potential swim spot. The river here is swimmable, but not that deep. Its suitability depends on

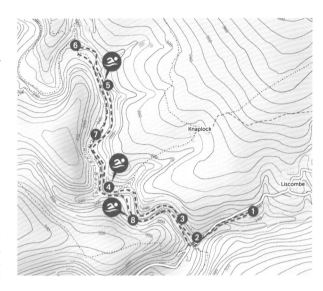

how high the river is. It's definitely worth a look, we had a lovely swim here when it was quite low.
0.3 miles

6 At this point you need to ford the river from a beachy area to a stand of imposing beech trees on the other side with a path between them. After fording the river, turn left and walk across a meadow, go through a gate and rejoin the path as its heads uphill. If the river is too high to ford, you have two choices, one short and one long. You can simply go back and cross the footbridge you passed earlier, near point 4, to walk back along the other bank. Or you can walk on along the river to Withypool and pick up the Exe Valley Way, which takes you back down to Tarr Steps on the western side but unfortunately away from the bank

of the river; this doubles the length of the walk.
0.6 miles

7 You reach a fork. Bear right here following the blue bridleway arrow; the path ascends and you go through a wooden gate before descending down to the river again. You pass the footbridge on your left and shortly after this find the main swimming spot (opposite point 4). Carry on walking with the river on your left.
0.6 miles

8 You reach another potential swim spot. It's not as deep as the main one but still fun for a plunge. Carry on walking by the river until you reach Tarr Steps; cross them and retrace your steps to the car park.
0.9 miles

Walk 21

DULVERTON, BRUSHFORD AND EXEBRIDGE

A lovely day out, walking from Somerset over the border into Devon, swimming in numerous beautiful pools on the Barle and Exe rivers, and getting the bus back. Please note that at the time of writing there are no buses on Sundays.

This is the perfect walk for a warm summer's day; there are plenty of swimming opportunities where you can cool down. In fact, last time we were here it was so hot we walked in our swimsuits, which made frequent dipping super-easy. The adventure starts in the ancient market town of Dulverton ❶, often referred to as 'the capital of Exmoor'. It is home to the headquarters of Exmoor National Park Authority, which was created in 1954 to "conserve and enhance the natural beauty, wildlife and cultural heritage of the National Park and to promote opportunities for the understanding and enjoyment of (its) special qualities." There is a visitor centre in the main shopping street where you can pick up lots of useful information and speak to their knowledgeable staff.

You can't miss the unusual town hall, which has a grand, arched double staircase leading to a covered balcony. It was originally built as a market house in 1866; the arches on the ground floor were open to allow the easy access of goods and people. However, the market went into decline soon after, and the building eventually found new use as a town hall. In 1930 alterations were made, including what the architectural historian Nikolaus Pevsner described as "a very elegant porch and stairway", and it feels like the perfect stage for some politician to broadcast their message to the world, or, at least, the public of Dulverton. These days, the building is used for a host of community activities: films and plays are shown; there are clubs and classes including line dancing, choirs and keep fit; it also has a charity shop run by volunteers to raise money for the building.

INFORMATION

DISTANCE: 4.5 miles
TIME: 4 hours
MAP: OS Explorer Map OL114 Exeter and the Exe Valley
START AND END POINT: Lion Stables car park in Dulverton (SS 914 278, TA22 9DW, What3Words: combines.slopes.denim)
PUBLIC TRANSPORT: the 25 bus from Taunton terminates at Dulverton; you will catch it back from Exebridge at the end of the walk
SWIMMING: Pools in the River Barle (SS 918 270 and SS 919 269), pools in the River Exe by Exebridge (SS 930 244 and SS 932 248)
REFRESHMENTS: The Anchor at Exebridge is perfectly placed at the end of the walk and has a lovely garden with tables right by the river (01398 323433, TA22 9AZ); there are lots of cafés and hostelries in Dulverton, including the fun Mad Hatter's Tea Room, which has excellent home-made cake (TA22 9HB)
EASIER ACCESS: Entry to the river Exe from the car park by the Anchor pub at Exebridge is really easy, with is a sloping shingly beach into the water.
NEARBY SWIM SPOTS: the River Barle at Tarr Steps, and the River Exe at the Community Orchard in Tiverton

The route heads down the main street towards the river, before turning left up Chapel Lane ❷. Just before Chapel Lane is an alleyway leading to the town's Catholic church, which was built in 1955 on the site of a stable. The area around it is rather dilapidated, but the church is worth a look as it is a perfect example of mid-20th-century design, with some lovely stained glass and a wooden crucifix above the altar by the controversial artist and letter carver Eric Gill.

Shortly after turning up Chapel Lane, you see the sad but still rather beautiful old Dulverton Laundry, with its elegant pale blue windows. It dates back to the late 18th or early 19th century, and over its history was variously a woollen mill, a factory producing silk, crêpe and lace, and, most recently, a laundry. An inventory from 1859 suggests that at that time it employed 70 workers operating at least 11 looms powered by a large water wheel. It was sold at auction in 2018 but, so far, the new owner does not appear to have started renovation work.

The walk continues along the lane past some pretty cottages and the local sports field, before the lane dwindles into a well-used track. You're now walking on the Exe Valley Way, which you'll follow all the way to Exebridge. Shortly after passing the water treatment works ❸, look for a gateway on the right onto a path down to the river, where you'll immediately find a little 'beach' ❹. It is easy to wade in to the water from here, but we prefer to get in slightly further down, just above Beasley Weir ❺ where the water is deeper, although the access down the bank is a bit steeper there. This is a beautiful, deep stretch of river, and makes a really decent swim; you can swim upstream for about 200 metres and float back down with the current. As with all weirs, stay

well clear of the structure itself, as the current can speed up and you risk being swept over.

On the Ordnance Survey map, the weir is described as a 'salmon trap' but this is in fact a fish pass, which enables salmon to get up the river via a series of shallow steps. The pass was considerably improved in 2015, when a hydropower scheme with an Archimedes screw was built; you can see the timber-clad building that houses the machinery on the other side of the river. Fascinatingly, this was not a new development at all. The weir was actually first built back in 1909 for a new hydroelectric plant, one of a number set up on Exmoor around that time by people who wanted to generate their own electricity. There was no national grid back then, so if locals wanted power they had to create it themselves. Beasley Weir, or Beasley Power Station as it was known, was built to supply power to the Dulverton Electric Light Company, and continued doing so until the setting up of the national grid in 1938.

The walk continues along a beautiful stretch of river brimming with pools and small rapids. There are lots of spots which are great for paddling, and also a few more places you can dip. You reach a bridge with a lodge house and the remains of gateposts over to the left ❻ which mark an old entrance to Pixton Park, a stately home lived in by a succession of powerful families including the Aclands and the Herberts and, during the Second World War, the writer Evelyn Waugh. Today, it is still a private home.

From here, the route continues alongside the river, before leaving it to enter the village of Brushford ❽. Until Victorian times this was a sleepy hamlet consisting of a church and a few cottages, but in the 1870s it suddenly woke up with the arrival of the railway. A station

opened here in 1873, called Dulverton even though the town is about ❷ miles away. No one seems to know why the station was built here, in Brushford, and there were doubtless many confused passengers who arrived thinking they were in Dulverton, only to have to fork out for a hansom cab for the rest of the journey. Henry Herbert, the 4th Earl of Carnarvon, who lived at Pixton Park, built a hotel to take advantage of the resulting tourism boom, and named it after himself. The Carnarvon Arms Hotel became something of a legend, and Evelyn Waugh's granddaughter Sophia Watson wrote a book about it called *A Lazy Contentment*, with stories of celebrity visitors including Alfred, Lord Tennyson, General Eisenhower and even the Beatles. The boom didn't last forever: the railway was shut in 1966 as part of the infamous Dr Beeching's cuts, the hotel closed in 2002 after being hit hard by the 2001 foot and mouth outbreak, and the village has returned to being a quiet backwater.

Once out of Brushford, the scenery changes as you start to ascend along the side of Hulverton Hill ⓫, and there are wonderful views of the surrounding countryside and the valley down to your right. You pass through a wood before descending to a rather romantic but ramshackle old barn with a red corrugated iron roof. Here, the route takes you left along a lane through an ancient farmstead called Riphay Barton, before turning right into the main road for a short distance, before reaching Exebridge ⓭.

The bridge itself straddles the border between Somerset and Devon and is quite elegant, with three arches. As you cross it, look over to the left and down and you will see a lovely pool where the river is joined by a small stream; this is the next

swimming spot. Just over the bridge is the historic Anchor Inn, the scene of a local legend about a 17th-century Devon highwayman, Tom Faggus; he was known as the 'Robin Hood of Exmoor' for his preference for only robbing wealthy travellers, and makes an appearance in RD Blackmore's Exmoor novel *Lorna Doone*. After a lifetime of evading capture, he was apparently caught in a sting in this very pub, when he gave money to a beggar who turned out to be a constable in disguise. He was arrested and sent to the gallows in Taunton.

Opposite the Anchor is a large free car park, where you can access the river, which is now the Exe rather than the Barle. The two rivers converge a short distance upstream, but unfortunately there is no public access to the confluence. On the bank here you will find a stony beach, from where you can get into the water. There is a nice, deep area where a stream on the other side joins the river; you might notice a sudden change of temperature where the two meet; the stream is much warmer!

You can finish the walk at this point, or extend it along the river to another swimming spot (14), dominated by an enormous sandstone and brick pillar which towers over one side. This is all that is left of the railway bridge that used to carry trains to Dulverton. The river here is not that deep, but it's good if you need a dip to cool down, and an interesting spot to see just about the only remains of the railway line that was part of life here for nearly a century. After a swim, retrace your steps to the Anchor, from where you can catch the bus back to Dulverton. If you still want another swim once you're back there, it's possible to get in just upstream of the bridge, a popular place for paddling and launching canoes.

1 Turn left out of the Lion Stables car park along the High Street.
0.1 miles

2 Just before Paul Hardy antiques, turn left up Chapel Street. Follow the road as it bears round to the left, passing the old Dulverton Laundry building on the right and then the Congregational Chapel on the right. Continue along the lane passing the sports field on your right, and keep following it as it becomes a track.
0.2 miles

3 Pass a water treatment works on your right. Shortly after, look for a gate on the right. Turn right through the gate, along the right-hand side of the field, and follow the path down towards the river.
0.2 miles

4 You arrive at the river where there is a sandy beach, an easy place to get in for a swim. We prefer to swim from point 5, a little further on, as it is deeper, but the access is a little more difficult there, you have to scramble down the bank. You can swim from here all the way down to point 5.
0.2 miles

5 Just before a weir, you will see an access point to the river down the bank. The water is lovely and deep here and you can swim for quite some distance upstream towards point 4 before swimming back. After, carry on walking with the river on your right. From this point onwards there are lots of paddling and dipping spots in the

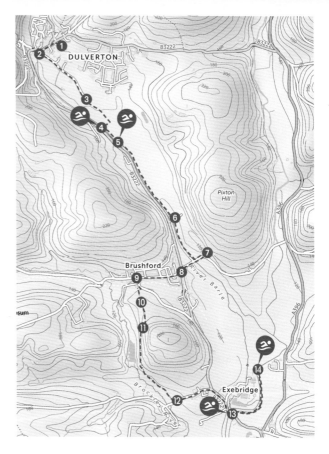

river, but none as deep and long as the stretch between points 4 and 5.
0.5 miles

6 You reach a stone bridge over the river on the right and a stone lodge building on the left. Follow the path past the bridge on your right and the lodge on your left, and then bear right in the field to pick up the path along the river

again (the main footpath continues ahead to your left). Keep walking with the river on your right, until the end of the field where the riverside path bears left and rejoins the main path.
0.3 miles

7 Go through the metal gate onto the road and turn right. Cross the river.
0.1 miles

⑧ At the main road turn left and then immediately right up Brushford New Road. Pass Nicholas Close on the right, and Brushford Parish Hall on the left.
0.2 miles

⑨ Just after Jubilee Gardens on the right, turn left at the crossroads and cross the bridge. Pass a house called Ellesboro on the right and follow the road as it bends to the left. Just after the bend, turn right through a metal gate into a field, following the public bridleway sign. Bear right, walking along the hedge on the right-hand side of the field for about 150 metres.
0.1 miles

⑩ You reach a metal gate on the right. Go through here and turn immediately left. You are now walking uphill alongside the hedge on your left.
0.1 miles

⑪ You reach the wood. Bear right into the wood and start walking downhill with the wooded hill on your left. As you leave the wood, ignore a track to your left and keep on the main path, walking towards a ruined barn ahead. Pass the barn and carry on following the main track. You will notice a marshy area to your right.
0.6 miles

⑫ At the road, turn left. Pass Brocksbridge Cottage on the left and follow the road through Riphay Barton, a collection of farm buildings. At the T-junction turn right, following the sign for Bampton and Exeter. You are now on the main road for a short distance, so take care. Pass the village sign for Exebridge.
0.4 miles

⑬ Cross the bridge over the Exe to the Anchor pub, turn left into the pub car park and bear left to find a good swimming spot just above the bridge. After, go back to the car park and look for the gate into the field to the right of the river. Go through and walk with the river on your left.
0.5 miles

⑭ You reach the remains of a railway bridge on the right, a large arch. This is the final swim spot on the walk. After, retrace your steps to the Anchor pub, where you can catch the bus back to Dulverton.
0.5 miles

Walk 22

THE TAW TUMBLE

An aquatic adventure along the beautiful River Taw, starting with a gorgeous walk from a quaint Devon village. Swim shoes are a must as the river is rocky, and a dry bag to carry your stuff is also a good idea though not vital.

INFORMATION

DISTANCE: 6 miles
TIME: 5 hours
MAP: OS OS Explorer 127 South Molton & Chulmleigh
START AND END POINT: Chittlehampton free car park (SS 636 255, EX37 9QL, What3Words: diamonds.defensive.humble)
PUBLIC TRANSPORT: The 859 bus operates between South Molton and Chittlehampton Mondays to Saturdays. The 658 bus between West Buckland and Barnstaple calls at Chittlehampton on Tuesdays and Fridays
SWIMMING: Railway bridge at Umberleigh (SS 609 240) and Taw Tumble near footbridge (SS 610 244)
REFRESHMENTS: the Bell Inn at Chittlehampton is a bit of a local legend with a warm welcome and a lovely garden (01769 540368, EX37 9QL); Chittlechatter Stores is the village shop, which also has a daytime café serving sandwiches and cakes (01769 540693, EX37 9QN)
EASIER ACCESS: The first swim spot by the railway bridge is a short walk from the road and parking by the school, and you can walk into the water with no drop from the bank. Swim shoes are a must, as you have to wade to the swim spot.

This is a really great day out, especially in hot weather, because there is a large stretch of river that you can swim, wade and scramble through, which makes for enormous fun. The 'Taw Tumble' as we've called it, is also possible in other (more usual British) weather conditions, but it would be advisable to wear a wetsuit for warmth and protection. However, it's important to note that you should refrain from doing this in October, November and December (when you probably wouldn't want to anyway) because this is spawning time for the salmon and sea trout that frequent this river. They lay their eggs in the gravel on the river bed, which must not be disturbed.

Alternatively, you can simply swim in various pools at certain points on the walk, getting out in between. Again, when entering the river in the late autumn months do not step in any gravel, but make your way in by treading on solid rock.

The walk starts in the unspoilt village of Chittlehampton ❶; as well as being very pretty, this has the rare bonus of a free car park in the main central square. The whole place feels impossibly picturesque: it's full of old cob-walled, thatched cottages, the square is bordered by a beautiful church and a pub, and there's even an iron Victorian water pump in the middle. It feels like a sleepy backwater, but only a hundred years ago it was a busy community, with bakers, sweetshops, farriers, garages and ironmongers, and apparently, at one stage, eight alehouses.

Now, of course, times have changed, and most people who live here don't work here too, but there is a range of housing, from social to privately owned, and an impression that this is still a

vibrant community. There is a village shop, which also operates as a café, and the whole place feels really friendly.

From the square, the route goes left out of the car park past the pub and then turns immediately right down a path and into a field. Last time we visited there was a notice on the gate warning us of a bull there; we walked past him without a problem. Another time, he might not be in the field, but be aware that he might be (there should always be a sign on the gate telling you this). If this concerns you, this section can be avoided by walking along the quiet local roads for the first stretch instead. More details in the directions.

There's a little more walking on a very quiet road, passing a small hamlet around Ambow Farm, before you leave the tarmac and pick up a track through fields ❸. You rejoin a minor road for a short distance, before ending up in Pitt Wood ❻. The route descends through the trees, which are mostly pines; in the autumn, look out for fungi, including prized chanterelles. You also might see some rather wonderful wooden constructions, like elegant shelters, that someone has made in the trees. Once out of the wood, you head downhill through a field before emerging through South Nethercleave, in Umberleigh ❼.

Walking very briefly on the main road, you pass an unusual red-and-white wooden building. This is the Church of the Good Shepherd, which was originally built in 1874 by the local vicar, the Rev Robert Trefusis, for workers on the Great Western Railway. Sadly, at the time of writing, the building, which is owned by the Church of England, is in a very poor state of repair, and local worshippers are meeting elsewhere.

After passing the church, you soon meet the river. The route heads left, upstream, shortly passing under Black Bridge, which carries the Tarka Line between Exeter and Barnstaple. This section of the railway opened in 1854 as the North Devon Railway. It was renamed the Tarka line over a hundred years later, after the success of Henry Williamson's book *Tarka the Otter*, in which the River Taw was Tarka's home and playground.

The Taw rises on Dartmoor and is one of Devon's longest rivers, at 45 miles long. At this point it is still freshwater, but about 4 miles downstream from here it becomes tidal, and shortly after that, joined by another great river, the Torridge, it empties into the sea at Bideford Bay. Its catchment covers over 745 square miles of North Devon, and it is home to many species including otters, salmon, sea trout, brown trout, eels, and lampreys. It's famous for its game fishing, so the River Taw Fisheries and Conservation Association works hard to protect the river, which is always at risk from threats like pollution and flooding.

The first swim spot ❽ is to be found just after you've walked under the bridge. Standing on the bank, looking right towards the bridge, the river is quite shallow. But there is a deeper 20-metre stretch to the left, by the opposite bank. Wade in from the entry point, where there are a few rocks, straight over to the other side. Walk upstream for a short distance and you will soon find you are out of your depth and can have a lovely swim, looking up towards the elegant road bridge over the river at Umberleigh in the distance. Looking downstream you will see the railway bridge, and you can wave to the passengers in the trains as they pass; last time we were there two or three trains went by.

After a dip here, you retrace your steps back under the bridge, and carry on walking with the river on your left. After crossing a footbridge, you will find the entrance to the start of the Taw

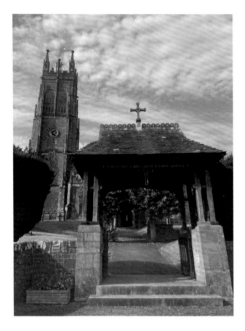

(There are also ladders on the left, but they lead onto private land so should not be used.) There is another deep stretch just after the ladder on the right. After, return to the ladder and get out.

If you don't wish to swim the whole stretch, you can either get in after the footbridge **9** and swim in the pool just downstream from there, or else walk down to the ladder **10** and swim in the pool below there. The pool at **9** is the one we recommend, as you don't have the hassle of climbing down the ladder to reach it.

Last time we did this walk it was a blistering hot day, and we enjoyed seeing a couple of pairs of fellow swimmers out doing the same 'river run' as us. One, with goggles, had his face permanently in the water, gliding along, obviously enjoying the beautiful sight of the rocky river bed and its weeds, all illuminated by sunlight bouncing through the water. It really is an idyllic way to spend some time, one feels as though one is in a scene from *Wind in the Willows*.

At the ladder get-out point, the route (sadly) heads away from the river, crossing a boardwalk, and passing through a hamlet called Hoe. It then ascends through a field to Whey Farm, before picking up a minor road which takes you all the way back to Chittlehampton.

Once back in the village, it's worth a small detour to visit Roger Cockram Ceramics, which you can find by turning right at the first crossroads; the studio is about 150 metres down the road on the right. Roger is a renowned craftsman who works mainly with porcelain, and his work is in both private and public collections around the world. He is particularly fascinated by water and the sea, and many of the works are beautiful shades of blue and green. The studio is open Monday to Friday; it's a good idea to ring before visiting (01769 540420).

Tumble **9**. There's a gap in the hedge on the left; walk through it and you will find a rocky area leading down to the water. From here, after a short wade, you can swim for a decent stretch of about 300 metres, and get out at a fisherman's ladder further down **10**. If you have a dry bag you can carry your stuff with you in the water; otherwise get a fellow walker to carry it or simply walk back to the entry point.

The water is quite shallow at the entry point, which is why you need swim shoes to protect your feet, as the river bed is rocky and can also be slippery. Head downstream and you will very soon reach a nice long stretch on your right where it's deep enough to swim. It becomes shallow again and you will see a ladder coming up on the right.

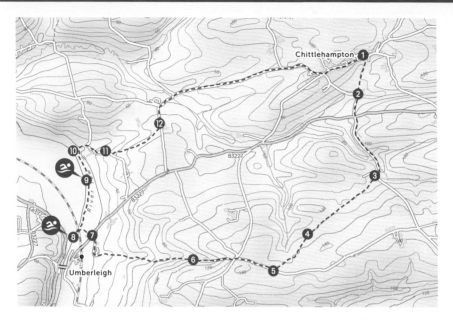

❶ From the car park, with your back to the church, turn left into the road passing The Bell Inn on your right. Just after the Bell and a white house called the Belfry, turn right. Follow the path into a field. (NB when we visited there was a bull in the field; there was a sign on the gate to alert us). Follow the path as it bears right across the field. At the end go through a gate and under a passageway under the gable end of a house to emerge onto a road. If the bull is a problem, turn right out of the car park along the main village street instead, and then turn left at the crossroads (signed for Chittlehamholt) and walk to the house where the end of the footpath is signed.
0.3 miles

❷ From the path turn left on the road. Shortly you reach a crossroads; go straight on here. The road heads downhill and you pass Ambow Farm on the right. The road starts to ascend again and bears right.
0.6 miles

❸ Take the public footpath signed off the road to the right. There is a private driveway just before it to the right; do not go down here. The public footpath is a track for a while; follow this until it ends by turning right into a field. From here keep going straight across the corner of the field you are in, heading for the stile opposite. Cross the stile and walk along the left-hand edge of the field by the hedge.
0.6 miles

❹ You reach an odd junction of gates. Go through the first metal five-bar gate; you are then faced with two more gates, left and right. Go through the left-hand seven-bar metal gate, and walk ahead on the right-hand side of the field, with the hedge on your right. Halfway along the field you will find a stile on your right. Cross over it and bear right, passing a barn on your left. Head for the gate to the right of the barn where there is a large oak tree. Go through the gate and walk straight ahead towards a gate into the road.
0.3 miles

❺ At the road turn right. You then reach a T-junction. Turn left here and then immediately right down a driveway with a public footpath sign and (confusingly) a sign saying PITT

Private Road. Don't worry: this is the route, and is a public footpath. Follow it downhill and pass a house on your right.
0.5 miles

6 Just past the driveway to the house on the right, keep going straight and you will reach a stile and gate into the wood. Cross into the wood and descend, following the path. As the path emerges from the wood, follow it as it bends right to follow the edge of the field. Go through a metal gate and keep walking straight ahead. Emerge in a small collection of houses and pick up a small lane. Pass stables on your left and then a children's playground.
0.8 miles

7 At the road turn right and then immediately left, onto a public footpath. Follow it as it bends left past the old wooden chapel and then right, heading for the river. When you reach the river, turn left and pass under the railway bridge.
0.2 miles

8 Just after the railway bridge you will find the first swim spot. The deepest stretch is off the opposite bank to the left. Wade in from the entry point to the other side, and then take a few steps upstream. The deep bit is about 20 metres long. After, retrace your steps back under the railway bridge and continue walking with the river on your left. Cross a footbridge.
0.1 miles

9 Shortly after crossing the footbridge, you will see a hole in

the hedge to your left which leads down to a stony access point to the river. This is the start point for what we've dubbed the Taw Tumble. You can get into the water here (swim shoes are essential) and swim and scramble your way down for about 300 metres through various pools and shallower bits to a point with a ladder further down (see main text for more detail). After, you can walk back to retrieve your stuff or any non-swimmers can carry it and meet you at the exit point. Whether walking or swimming, the route continues through another field, where it leaves the river.
0.3 miles

10 Go through a gate which takes the path away from the river to the right. Cross a boardwalk and keep walking ahead. Turn right into a lane and follow it as it wiggles through the hamlet of Hoe.
0.3 miles

11 Just after leaving the hamlet, there is a public footpath off the road over a stile to the left. Take this and head across the field slightly to the right uphill, towards a gateway you can see in the hedge opposite. Cross a stile through the gateway and head across the next field towards the houses. At the field corner, turn left through a metal gate following a yellow footpath arrow, go over a stile and turn right.
0.4 miles

12 You reach a T-junction with Whey Farm opposite. Turn left and follow the lane downhill and to the right, following signs for Cobbaton and Chittlehampton. Cross a stone bridge and continue straight on for Chittlehampton. Ascend the hill until you reach the village at a crossroads. Turn left following signs for Filleigh until you reach the car park (or make a short diversion right for the pottery studio).
1.5 miles

Walk 23

RIVER TORRIDGE AND TORRINGTON COMMONS

A beautiful day out with lots of walking by the River Torridge and several swimming opportunities; bring water shoes to protect your feet, as the bottom of the river is stony.

INFORMATION

DISTANCE: 5 miles
TIME: Allow 6 hours
START AND END POINT: South Street car park, Great Torrington (SS 494 189, EX38 8AA, What3Words: waged.gravy.rudder)
PUBLIC TRANSPORT: Great Torrington is well served by buses, including the 5B between Exeter and Barnstaple, the 317 between Bideford and Okehampton and the 71 between Barnstaple and Holsworthy
SWIMMING: Ladies Pool (SS 495 188), pool with rope swing (SS 491 188), pool below weir (SS 483 188) and Rothern Bridge (SS 479 197)
REFRESHMENTS: The Puffing Billy café is halfway along the walk and serves snacks including soup and chips (01805 623050, EX38 8JD).
EASIER ACCESS: You can park by New Bridge (SS 500 184), with a walk of about 10 minutes to Ladies Pool. You still have to walk down a few steps to reach the river bank, and take a couple of steps down from the bank itself to get into the water. The pool at Rothern Bridge is also quite easy, about a minute's walk from parking by the Puffing Billy café. You can walk down a gentle slope from the bank into the water.
NEARBY SWIM SPOTS: The River Torridge has a small swimmable stretch upstream at Beaford Woods (SS 544 141). Park at Beaford Bridge and cross the bridge heading north and uphill past Beaford Mill before taking the public footpath to the right. Walk down through the woods to a swimmable stretch where the footpath joins the river

lthough the walk starts in a pretty Devon market town, today's outing does not feel like an urban experience. For most of the day you will be exploring woods and meadows. The other wonderful thing about this route is the amount of time you get to spend walking beside the lovely River Torridge; such a long stretch of public footpath by a river is not that common in this part of Devon. There are also numerous places to swim on the route, which is a total joy.

The adventure starts in the mundane surroundings of a car park ❶, but it is a car park with a difference: it has the most incredible view over the river below and countryside beyond, stretching as far as the eye can see. Torrington is perched on top of a huge inland cliff, with, perhaps ironically, the car park having one of the best outlooks. You might notice two long, thin fields in the distance. These are the typical fields of medieval times, and survived because there was a leper colony in Taddiport on the other side of the river, away from the main population. There were still seven of these small strips in the 19th century.

From the car park, you step through a stone archway, leaving the town behind and emerging on a large, steep and beautiful wooded hillside. This area is part of Great Torrington Common. The town has 365 acres of common land, mostly on the western side (which we will come to later), which was given to it by the lord of the manor in 1194. All this land has been owned and looked after by local people ever since, with an elected Committee of Conservators.

You'll soon pass the Waterloo Monument ❷, a stone obelisk built by local women in memory of their husbands and sons who

died in the famous battle of 1815. Unusually, its inscription contains three exclamation marks, saying 'PEACE TO THE SOULS OF THE HEROES!!!' At the time of writing, the Conservators are raising money to restore the monument, which is starting to deteriorate. The walk continues high on the common, before dropping down beside a pretty stream known as Lady Wash ❸. Legend has it that young girls would rise early on May Day to wash their faces in it, hoping this would make them especially beautiful – or perhaps it was just somewhere women came to do the laundry. Either way, it is very picturesque, tumbling down through cascades and pools lined with ferns and mosses.

At the bottom, you turn right ❹ and pick up the main path along the River Torridge, which you'll be walking along for the next couple of miles or so. You're now on the route of the old Rolle Canal, which was built in the 1820s to transport limestone from the port at Bideford to kilns inland, where it was processed and used as fertiliser. It closed around 50 years later, with the coming of the railway, and was almost entirely filled in. We'll find out more about it later on in the walk.

You can't mistake the first swim spot, Ladies Pool ❺, which is bordered by a large concrete platform. Local people have swum here for at least a century, and the platform was built in the late 1920s with money raised by public subscription. There is still a plaque on it today which tells us it was provided 'by the women of Great Torrington….1927–28'. Apparently there used to be a changing shed as well. Metal rings on the front of the concrete suggest that perhaps ladders once provided direct access into the water. Sadly, that is no longer the case, and the best place to get in is to the left of the platform, where someone has helpfully placed a bit of rock to ease the way. Do wear shoes with a firm sole to protect your feet, as the bottom of the river is very stony, with some big rocks which can stub your toes if you're not careful.

After a dip, continue on beside the river, where there are three swimming options (points ❻, ❽ and ❿). The first has a rope swing and is just a short distance on from Ladies Pool, while the second is downstream of a large weir. The final spot is a little further on at Rothern Bridge by the Puffing Billy café. If it's a hot day, you could consider walking in your swim stuff to maximise dipping opportunities! After crossing the road at Taddiport Bridge ❼ the route continues along the river past a large weir ❽, below which it is possible to swim. You eventually leave the waterside (temporarily, you'll be glad to hear), passing under an old iron railway bridge before joining the Tarka Trail at the site of the former Torrington railway station ❾. This is the perfect place for both another swim and a pit stop, with the Puffing Billy café in the old station building and Torrington Cycle Hire behind it both offering refreshments.

The swim spot ❿ is about a minute's walk from the Puffing Billy café. To find it, stand with your back to the café and follow the road downhill to the right. It then bends to the left and reaches Rothern Bridge, which is now a dead end. Cross the bridge and turn immediately left down a little boardwalk to the river (take care as it's a bit slippery).

This lovely section of the Torridge is very popular with locals for both paddling and swimming. Rothern Bridge dates back to the early 15th century and is a rare medieval survivor. At one point it was one of only two river crossings in the area; in 1928 when the bridge next to it (which now carries the traffic) was built, the authorities suggested the old bridge should be demolished. However, there was an outcry and it was kept.

After a swim, the walk continues along the Tarka Trail. This 180 mile route – which you can walk or cycle – was created about 40 years ago. Much of it is on disused railway lines, as we see here, in the shape of a figure of eight that takes in Barnstaple, Bideford, Okehampton, Lynton and Braunton. Torrington Station opened in 1872 (interestingly, the authorities didn't think it was important enough to include the 'Great') but was closed as part of massive railway cuts in 1965. This section is popular with cyclists, being smooth and flat, so stay alert to avoid collisions!

After a short distance you turn off the trail ⓫, to pick up a permissive path which rejoins the river.

You soon come across steps on the left which take you down to the water, but the bank is quite high so swimming here is a bit of a challenge. Another set of steps takes you back up to the path, where you are again following the course of the Rolle Canal, with the river down below to your left. As you can see from some of the remaining walls, the canal was narrow. Small 'tub' boats were tied together in groups of three or four and pulled by horses on a towpath. Limestone was brought in, and on the return journey the boats carried goods such as wool and pottery back to Bideford, which was still a major regional port at the time. At the end of the permissive path, you walk underneath the Roving Bridge ⓬, which let a horse to cross from one side of the canal to the other without being unharnessed from the boat. It is pretty narrow, considering both the boats and the horses had to get through it. There are several information boards along this section of the walk giving more details about the industrial history.

The route turns back along the Tarka Trail, crossing the river again with wonderful views both up and downstream, before heading away from the river and through a meadow with a pond. Shortly after, you enter Great Torrington Common again ⓭, with its numerous quirkily named paths, including Barmaids Path and Old Maid's Walk. You pass a pretty stream with a picnic bench beside it ⓮ which is pleasant place to stop, particularly if you have young children who will enjoy paddling here.

The walk leaves the common past the cemetery, and you emerge back in town in the glamorous surroundings of Lidl car park. It's worth exploring around the town centre before you leave, as it has a charming pannier market, an arts centre and museum. You may notice banners in the shops proclaiming "us be plaised to zee 'ee" – so you should have a warm welcome.

1 From the car park, follow the stone wall along the eastern side by the library and community centre. At the end, go through an archway and turn left. Follow the path past a row of benches, ignoring a path which switchbacks down to the right. Keep following the path and then bear right downhill.
0.3 miles

2 You reach the Waterloo monument. From here, bear left following the path until you're nearly at the road.
0.1 mile

3 At the stream, turn right, going down a few steps to join the path downhill with the stream on your left.
0.1 mile

4 You arrive at a T-junction of paths with a big metal drain cover. Turn right here; you are now walking with the River Torridge on your left.
0.3 miles

5 You will see some steps to your left, and a path joining from the right. Go down the steps and continue along the river for a very short distance to find the first swim spot at Ladies Pool. There is a large concrete platform by the water. After a dip, carry on walking alongside the river.
0.2 miles

6 You reach another swim spot; this one has a wooden swing. Carry on walking next to the river

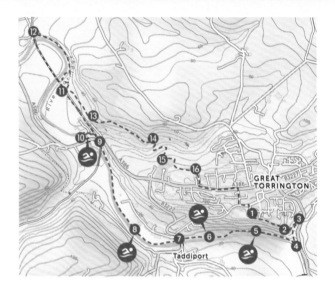

bank. You come to a meadow; keep following the river.
0.2 miles

7 You arrive at Taddiport Bridge. Cross over the road and continue walking with the river on your left. You pass a large weir.
0.3 miles

8 You reach another dipping spot just by a stile. Keep following the riverbank. Pass a sewage works on the right and keep following the river until you see some steps up to the right. Go up them and keep walking along the track.
0.6 miles

9 You reach a large metal overbridge which is the Tarka trail. Walk under it and continue uphill for about 75 metres before

turning right through an archway with a plaque saying 'Rolle Tunnel 1997'. Turn left following the unusual Sustrans sign for Bideford; you are now on the Tarka Trail. To find the next swim spot, at Rothern Bridge, head for the Puffing Billy café which you will see over to the left. Stand in front of the café with your back to it and follow the road downhill to the right, and then to the left as it crosses over Rothern Bridge. Turn immediately left after the bridge.
0.2 miles

10 After a swim in the river by Rothern Bridge, return to the Puffing Billy café and pick up the Tarka Trail behind it. Follow the trail in a north-westerly direction past an old railway carriage on the left.
0.4 miles

⓫ Turn right off the Tarka Trail by a bike stand and a sign saying Rolle Canal Walk. Bear left and follow the path. Very shortly on the left are some steps which take you on a little detour down to the river bank and then another set up again to the path. Continue walking with the river down below on your left. There are various little paths down to the river if you want to scramble down.
0.5 miles

⓬ You pass under the stone Roving Bridge and a sign explaining it on the left. Shortly after turn left through a gateway (at the time of writing the gate is broken) and rejoin the Tarka Trail, turning left back to point 11 (the start of the loop you've just done). Here turn

left off the Tarka trail and then right, following the sign for Reeds Field. You're now walking through a meadow. You pass a picnic bench and a pond on your right.
0.6 miles

⓭ Fork left, going uphill, by the cream house on the right. The path starts to ascend through the woods. You reach a crossroads of paths; turn right here following the sign for Old Bowling Green, and continue to follow signs for Old Bowling Green at the next two junctions.
0.4 miles

⓮ Cross a stream; shortly after on the left is a good place with a picnic table to stop for a rest, and where young children can have a paddle.

Just past the picnic area turn right (do not go straight on) and follow the path as it zig-zags uphill.
0.2 miles

⓯ You reach the churchyard wall. Turn left here, following the wall on your right, and follow the path around the cemetery wall, following signs for the Glass Factory.
0.2 miles

⓰ Just past a breeze-block wall turn right following the sign for the town centre. Emerge in Lidl car park and turn left into the main road. Turn right down White's Lane following sign for town centre car park. At the end of White's Lane turn left into South Street and the car park is shortly on your right.
0.5 miles

Walk 24

TAUNTON AND THE RIVER TONE CIRCULAR

A really picturesque walk through the heart of apple country, with several swimming opportunities in the River Tone, including one excellent community bathing facility.

INFORMATION

DISTANCE: 3 miles
TIME: Allow 3 hours
MAP: OS Explorer 128 Taunton & Blackdown Hills
START AND END POINT: Silk Mills Park & Ride (ST 208 254, TA1 5AA, What3Words: jars.best.cracks)
PUBLIC TRANSPORT: Taunton railway station is on the London–Penzance route, and a 15-minute walk from French Weir Park, a better place to start and end if travelling this way.
SWIMMING: Frieze Hill (ST 215 252), the Bathing Station at French Weir (ST 220 248)
REFRESHMENTS: The Weir café at COACH is a lovely spot for a drink and cake or a light lunch, looking over the River Tone and right by a swim spot (07592 392544, TA1 1AW). Rumwell Farm Shop and Café near Taunton is a great place to stock up on picnic supplies and has won multiple Taste of the West Awards (01823 461599, TA4 1EJ)
EASIER ACCESS: There is one disabled bay at COACH near the Bathing Station; Wood Street, Tangier and Enfield car parks are all a five-minute walk away. Whilst it is quite easy to get into the water from the wooden steps, it's a bit of a pull up to get yourself out again, so some assistance may be required.
NEARBY SWIM SPOTS: There is a nice pool in Norton Brook, on the other side of the main road from the park and ride (ST 205 253)

Today's walk starts at Silk Mills Park & Ride ❶, which while not being that glamorous, is really convenient. There's free parking, toilets and even bike storage, and it's remarkable how soon after the start of the walk you feel you are right out in the countryside – within minutes you are in Silk Mills Nature Reserve ❷. The area takes its name from Taunton's 18th-century silk spinning industry, built on its success as a prosperous wool-processing town as far back as the 13th century. The nature reserve was created as flood management and landscaping after the development of the park and ride, and provides a wonderful mixture of woodland and grassland alongside the River Tone ❸, where we will be walking today.

After following a path alongside a wheat field bordered with cow parsley and daisies, you reach the river and the first swim opportunity at an area called Frieze Hill ❹. There's an entry point on the right at a gap in the hedge, by a willow tree which makes an eerie creaking noise as its branches rub together. There's a lovely long stretch to swim in here, and you can either swim upstream and float back down under the marvellous canopy of oak, alder and sycamore trees, or swim downstream and then back up against the current. We did the latter right down as far as the bridge and then got a bit of a workout returning to the start.

According to local swimmers, white hawthorn blossoms with their spicy almond-like scent coat the river in the spring, while in the autumn it's not unusual to see apples floating downstream. We are, of course in the heart of Somerset, famous for its apple orchards and cider. You might also be fortunate enough to spot the electric blue of a kingfisher, a coot with its black body and

white forehead or even a sand martin in the spring, returning from wintering in Africa. The town name is derived from 'Town on the River Tone' or 'Tone Town', so it really is all about the river.

The route passes over a wooden bridge ❺ and continues along the river on the other side. It's worth exploring some of the small paths that lead off to the Tone, as there are other potential swim spots, and an area that's nicknamed 'the mangrove swamp' by local swimmers because of the exposed roots of the trees. The walk passes down through Longrun Meadow, which forms an important part of Taunton's flood defences. It is looked after by a friends' group with the aim of providing a high-quality green space for leisure and recreation. This includes managing the land in an environmentally sensitive way to increase the diversity of flora and fauna. A number of activities take place here weekly, including running, orienteering, cycling, kayaking and dog walking. Look out for the large open sided oak barn that has a real Amish feel.

There's an enormous pipe that crosses the river on your left, which we joked is a cider pipeline providing an unlimited supply of the apple-based beverage for locals. The walk then crosses back over the river via another foot bridge ❻ and into a small community park called French Weir (the weir is downriver just to your right). A weir has existed here since the 13th century, although destroyed by flooding and rebuilt many times over its history. In 1753 it was destroyed by a group of Taunton women who believed that the miller at the Town Mills was selling flour outside the area when they were experiencing food shortages. According to the website of the nearby Centre for Outdoor Activity and Community Hub (COACH)

"In 1862 the area which is now French Weir Park was rented to the parish of St James by John

Halliday and a bathing station was constructed below the weir. It had wooden changing cabins and a concrete waterfront. In 1864 the first annual swimming and diving competition took place. This was not without controversy, as the competitors (all male) swam naked. Complaints about nude bathing and bad language continued into the 1880s."

The council bought the park in 1893 and in the 1920s the bathing station below the weir was replaced by one above it, which boasted diving boards and grab chains along the river bank on the park side for swimmers to hold on to. While the chains have now gone, one of the large iron rings that held them can still be seen close to the bridge. Like many open-water bathing places, swimming in the river Tone went into sharp decline when the public baths at St James Street opened in 1928.

As you enter the park you will see the Weir Café and COACH building, which caters for people with a love for the outdoors and adventure sports. Past the end of the building you will reach some steps down to a wooden platform ❼ that provides access to a beautiful stretch of the river for various water sports activities, including swimming – indeed, you can swim all of the way to our first swim spot if you are feeling adventurous. It's still known locally as the Bathing Station, and is a popular swim spot with an active community of regular swimmers. It's a fantastic and forward-thinking community facility, and we'd love to see more of these platforms and access points across the UK.

The walk back follows a section of the Two Counties Way, a 56-mile trail that starts in Taunton, follows the route of the Grand Western Canal to Tiverton and then heads down the Exe Valley to Exeter. From there it follows the towpath of the Exeter Ship Canal past Powderham Castle to reach Starcross. It takes the average person around 22

hours to complete, and would make the ultimate wild swimming walk if you ever fancy a challenge.

Our walk takes you around between some houses and allotments and then into Frieze Hill Community Orchard, which has a fantastic history. The land was gifted to the council of Taunton by a local landowner called Henry Gribble Turner during the First World War. Concerned about food shortages, he wanted to provide a place where people could grow their own. Allotments were established on part of it, but the rest lay unused for many years following the war, until the community orchard was established. Today it contains more than 120 fruit trees, many gifted by local people,

with several heritage varieties like Dabinett and Kingston Black.

An Apple Day is held every October, and a Wassail in January. The latter sees The Lord of Misrule and the Wassail Princess and Prince pouring cider onto the tree roots and putting cider-soaked toast in the branches of the trees to ensure a good harvest. There is also singing, chanting and loud noise making, to wake up the trees to be fruitful for the year. It seems to work: apparently the orchard always has a bountiful harvest and the fruit is available for everyone to pick – so why not finish today's walk by enjoying some delicious fruit in Somerset, the heart of apple country?

1 With your back to the entrance to the car park, and the waiting room behind you, find the footpath at the north-east corner of the car park, which is ahead of you to the left. Follow the path into the Silk Mills Nature Reserve.
0.2 miles

2 At the big Silk Mills Nature Reserve sign turn right down a little path. You reach a gate and a stile. Turn left here, following the yellow arrow, and walk alongside the left-hand side of a field. Go through a metal gate.
0.3 miles

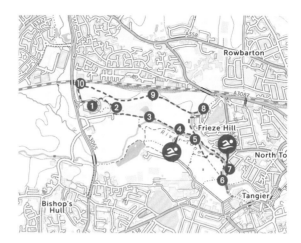

3 You reach an open gateway; bear slight right here and walk between two wooden posts ahead of you; the left-hand one has Silk Mills written on it. Follow the path with the river on your right.
0.2 miles

4 You reach the first swim spot; there is a clear gap in the hedge and a way down to the river. Have a dip here; there is a good long stretch and it gets deeper if you go left (downstream) or right (upstream.) After, carry on walking with the river on your right.
0.1 miles

5 You reach a wooden footbridge. Cross over and turn left, so the river is now on your left. There are a few places along here where you can get in for a dip. Follow the path through Longrun Meadow, and alongside the river.
0.4 miles

6 You reach another footbridge. Cross over and you will see the Weir café on your left. Walk past the café and turn immediately left. Pass the end of the building which says COACH on it, and look for the entry to the water on the left.
0.1 mile

7 You are at the Bathing Station swim spot. Sometimes the gate is closed, but it is still fine to go in. There are steps down and a wooden platform to access the water, and you can swim all the way up to the previous spot if you like. After a dip, go back to the path and turn left, walking with the river on your left. You pass a sign for Two Counties Way, and there is a small concrete wall between the path and the river. You reach the first footbridge again (point 5): here you could just retrace your steps, but to make the walk circular, bear right away from the river, walking between the houses

on your right and a field on your left. Follow the path as it turns right between two houses into a housing estate. At the road, turn left and follow the road bending right (Roughmoor Crescent). At the end of Roughmoor Crescent turn left into Home Cottages and follow the path past the end of the terraced houses.
0.5 miles

8 Turn left onto a path, heading west. You reach a sign for a community orchard. Go straight on.
0.3 miles

9 You reach a crossroads of paths. Go straight on here.
0.5 miles

10 You reach a metal gate with a stile beside it. Go through here and turn left, walking along a road that curves left back to the car park.
0.2 miles

Walk 25

TIVERTON FIGURE OF EIGHT

A great walk through the historic town of Tiverton learning about its wool and textile heritage, before enjoying two delicious dips in the River Exe; a long swim is possible if you take a towfloat for your stuff, or have a helpful friend to carry it!

INFORMATION

DISTANCE: 5 miles

TIME: Allow 3 hours

START AND END POINT: St Peter's Church, which has a few spaces parking spaces directly in front (SS 954 129, EX16 6RP, What3Words: token. cigar.feast)

PUBLIC TRANSPORT: The nearest train station is Tiverton Parkway; the 1a/b and 55 bus services run from Exeter

SWIMMING: The meadow (SS 947 133) and Tiverton Community Orchard (SS 953 129)

REFRESHMENTS: The Ducks Ditty Bar is a fully licensed canal barge moored at Tiverton Wharf (01884 253345, EX16 4HX). The 17th-century Mitre Inn is a stone's throw away from Tiverton in Witheridge, and with a big log fire and traditional décor it's a great spot for post-swim refreshments (01884 861263, EX16 8AE)

EASIER ACCESS: The swim spot at the orchard has parking spaces right next to it, and a small clamber down the river bank to get in. Another option would be to park at West Exe South Car park and enter the water at the slipway by the White Ball pub (SS 952 125)

NEARBY SWIM SPOTS: There are a couple of lovely pools in the Exe south of Tiverton, about an hour's walk on the public footpath which heads south out of the town following the river downstream. The first can be found by the remains of an old bridge. (SS 950 091 What3Words: amplified.pancake.laugh). The second is a little further on. It's fun to walk down the river to Bickleigh, and then get the bus back to Tiverton. There are also several swimming possibilities along the River Tone (see the Taunton chapter).

Today's walk starts right next to St Peter's Church ❶, which was described by Nikolaus Pevsner, author of the epic 46-volume *Buildings of England*, as "a gorgeously ostentatious display of civic pride." It is definitely worth a visit, as it also has an incredibly romantic claim to fame: its massive organ, which dates back to 1696, was used for the first performance of Mendelssohn's 'Wedding March' in 1847, and since then countless people around the world have walked down to aisle to the famous music.

The ornate Greenway Chapel and Greenway Porch were both paid for by Sir John Greenway, who was one of the wealthiest wool merchants in Tiverton – and he certainly wasn't shy about letting the world know who paid for the new additions. Over the inner doorway he included a carving of the Assumption that features him on one side of the Virgin Mary and his wife on the other side, kneeling in a suitably pious pose. In case anyone was in doubt, he also included his initials and the arms of the Drapers' Company.

Wool and textiles are going to become a theme of today's walk, and we soon join the Merchant's Trail ❷, marked by small brass plaques in the pavement. The walk passes through the Pannier Market, where markets have been held for over 1,000 years. A second hand goods market is held on Mondays, with a general market on Tuesdays, Fridays and Saturdays. There's also a popular night market on the first Saturday of the month from May to

September. The main Victorian pannier market building is a great place to pick up picnic items for the walk.

When you arrive at Gold Street, you will spot Greenway's Almshouses ❸, which were built in the 1520s. They were once the homes of five poor men who could no longer work, and each received eight pence a week on which to live. While not quite as altruistic as they first may seem (in return for the lodging they had to pray for the souls of John and Joan Greenway) the houses did leave a lasting legacy, providing a model that has been serving the town for over 500 years. Today they are part of the Tiverton Almshouses Trust, which has 83 almshouses providing high-quality homes with on-site warden support for local older people in need.

The walk continues through the town past historic buildings, independent shops, the impressive Tiverton Memorial Hall ❹ and St George's Church, which is considered one of the finest Georgian churches in Devon. Eventually you reach the River Exe: the town is named after the two fords that once crossed its two rivers – one across the Exe and the other across the Lowman. Over time, 'Two-Ford Town' has become Tiverton.

From the bridge, there's an iconic view up the river past the red-brick Bridge Guest House to St Peter's Church where we started the walk. On the other side of the bridge looking downriver, there's a slipway that you can use to get out of the water if you decide to swim down from the swim spot we will be visiting later.

Once over the bridge, the route bears right to pass one of the most famous buildings in Tiverton, the factory of Heathcoat Fabrics ❻. The firm has dominated life in the town for over two centuries, since an entrepreneur called John Heathcote bought the site to manufacture lace. He harnessed the power of the River Exe to power his newly-invented bobbin-net machines, as well as building a huge water wheel. His factory had around 300 machines, and around 2,000 employees worked for him there and at his iron-foundry. He was very popular, and later served the town as Member of Parliament for nearly 30 years.

Heathcote Fabrics went on to have an amazing history and remains an important producer of industrial fabrics today. It has produced everything from the veiling fabric for Queen Elizabeth's royal wedding in 1947 to the fabric for the parachute that successfully landed NASA's Perseverance Rover onto the surface of Mars in 2021 – so there is still a bit of Tiverton on the surface of that particular planet. You can visit the factory shop, which was formerly a school built by Heathcoat for the education of his workers' children in 1843. It was the first factory school in the west country, arising from his belief that children should not be employed until they could read and write – some 35 years before employing children under 10 was outlawed.

Walking down Leat Street, you will be able to see some of the houses built for the factory workers. The walk goes a bit urban for a short while, till we join a leat (a mill stream) and pass some allotments to enter a rather attractive meadow. Look out for the first swim spot ❽ soon after crossing the bridge. It's a lovely refreshing place for a dip although only about waist deep, so not suitable for a proper swim. The walk then continues along the leat to some old buildings that were once used to control the sluice gates that fed it. It's a really pretty spot overlooking the weir – just ignore the unattractive A361 you have to pass under to get there. Walking back along the River Exe there are several more potential dipping spots as you return around the meadow.

The walk takes a slightly unpromising route past a large Morrisons supermarket into the charming Tiverton Community Orchard ⓫, which was created in 2021–2022. It is home to more than 50 types of fruits and nuts, so you can find apples, plums, cherries, pears, damsons, blueberries, redcurrants, jostaberries, gooseberries, kiwi fruits, autumn olives and mulberries growing here, as well as nuts including almonds, sweet chestnuts and hazelnuts. The crops are free for everyone to take (at their own risk) but you are asked to pick lightly and leave some for others to enjoy. It's a fantastic creation, and better still, the orchard borders the river where you can take a dip. It is quite a surprise to find such a beautiful and lengthy stretch of water right in the middle of Tiverton, and swimming here gives a feeling of being truly 'away from it all' despite its proximity to so many commercial premises.

Several trees line the bank, including oak, black alder and sycamore. It is properly deep, and is a stunning spot for a proper swim, either up-river or downstream; you can swim quite a distance in either direction. As we swam downstream we found what looked like part of an old quay in the water, or perhaps a defensive wall for Tiverton Castle, which sits above. We also heard the bells of St Peter's ringing as we floated under the trees.

It's also possible to do a lovely 'A to B' swim here, if you have a tow bag in which to put your clothes or a willing walker to carry your stuff. You can swim all the way down river and under the bridge to the slipway we passed earlier on the walk (which is next to the White Ball Inn), a distance of about 500 metres.

Otherwise, after a dip, the walk takes a bit of an urban turn again, as it passes Morrisons and joins a path before a road ⓬ takes you back up to Tiverton Castle and the church ❶. Dating back to Norman Times, the motte was built in 1106 and extended in the 12th and 13th centuries. However, it fell to Parliamentarian troops who demolished it in the English Civil War, when an incredibly lucky shot hit the chain holding up the drawbridge. A manor house was later built in the grounds of the ruins; this is a private home, although the owners open it up to the public over the summer months. You can also buy a garden-only ticket that allows you to walk around the beautiful grounds and see the castle ruins.

As you'd expect, the castle is supposedly haunted by several ghosts, including two lovelorn phantoms from the 17th century. At that time the castle was the home of Sir Hugh Spencer, whose very beautiful daughter Alice had many admirers. Sir Hugh wanted Alice to marry an older friend of his called Sir Charles Trevor, who was known for his violent temper, but Alice was in love with Maurice Fortescue, the castle manager who was considered well below her social class. In a duel between the two, Maurice lost his life to the more experienced swordsman, who threw his rival's body in the Exe. In despair, Alice hurled herself into the river after her lover and drowned. Whenever the Exe is in flood, the two lovers can be seen walking arm in arm along the banks of the river, accompanied by Fortescue's faithful dog. Do keep an eye out for them if the river is in spate when you visit and you are unable to swim.

DIRECTIONS

1 From the car park by the church, walk south with the church wall on your right. Very shortly turn left into Newport Street, then take the first right just past the Baptist Church, following the sign for the short stay car park. At the end of the car park, with the Pannier Market hall straight ahead, turn left and pass through a pedestrianised area with shops. You might notice a small circular brass plaque in the pavement marking the Merchants' Trail, which you are now following.
0.2 miles

2 At the end of the pedestrianised area, turn right into Bampton Street (note the Merchant's Trail information panel on Bampton House on your left). At the end of Bampton Street, turn left into Gold Street opposite Banbury's department store, again following the brass plaque for the Merchants' Trail.
0.1 miles

3 Admire the beautiful old almshouses on the right, then retrace your steps to the junction with Bampton Street and carry on

straight ahead into another pedestrianised area. Pass the Tivoli Cinema on your left.
0.1 miles

4 At the Town Hall, bear right and downhill, past the Tiverton Memorial Hall, and cross the bridge. Note the slipway on the western side of the river, just below the bridge, where you can get out if you want to swim down from the Community Orchard later on in the walk. Pass the White Ball pub on your left
0.1 miles

5 At the roundabout turn right following West Exe North.
0.1 mile

6 You reach the entrance to the Heathcote Factory, where you can divert slightly to take a look and maybe patronise their shop, before continuing on the main road, which is called Leat Street. Pass Melbourne Street on your left and then a big roundabout on your right.
0.4 miles

7 Just after the Tiverton Dogs Centre turn right down a street called Loughborough. At the end turn left along the path with the leat on your right. By the allotments, turn right over a bridge – do not follow the public footpath sign to the left uphill – and enter a large meadow.
0.2 miles

8 The first swim spot is just on the right after the entrance to the meadow, after a redundant stile. There are also further swim spots further upstream, so you may prefer to walk the loop around the meadow

first to get the 'lie of the land'. After a dip, or just checking out the swim spot, head away from the river, walking north along the path beside the leat, with the leat on your left. Pass under the road bridge.
0.3 miles

9 You arrive at an old building and what looks like a quay, with a red metal post. There is a weir here, and it is a very beautiful spot to stop and have a breather before walking back along the other side of the meadow, with the river on your left. At point 8, retrace your steps to the roundabout.
0.6 miles

10 At the roundabout, turn left and cross the road bridge over the leat and the river. Turn right at the roundabout by Morrisons garage into Mountbatten Road. Pass the supermarket on your left and you will shortly after see the Community Orchard on your right, with a sign.
0.3 miles

11 In the orchard, find the river on your right; this is the next swim spot. It's possible to swim all the way from here down to the next bridge and get out up a slipway by the White Ball pub (point 4). After your swim, walk back along the road to the supermarket, following the 'pedestrian access' sign on the right. Turn past the front of the supermarket on your right. At the end of the building turn right, picking up a path which then immediately turns left beside a red brick wall.
0.3 miles

12 At the main road, turn right; this takes you back up to the church.
0.2 miles

KILLERTON AND THE RIVER CULM CIRCULAR

A beautiful walk around the outer edges of the historic Killerton estate, taking in an unusual chapel and two swims in the River Culm.

INFORMATION

DISTANCE: 4 miles
TIME: 3 hours
MAP: OS Explorer OL114 Exeter & the Exe Valley
START AND END POINT: Ellerhayes Bridge car park (SS 975 011, EX5 4PX, What3Words: milkman.decency. shameless) If this is full, there is another on the north-east side of the bridge; cross the bridge and turn immediately right to find it
PUBLIC TRANSPORT: The 675 bus between Exeter and Cheriton Fitzpaine calls at Ellerhayes but is a very limited service
SWIMMING: Pool near Ellerhayes Bridge (SS 974 013), Columbjohn Bridge (SX 957 997)
REFRESHMENTS: None on the walk. There is a coffee shop and a café at the National Trust at Killerton (01392 881345, EX5 3LE); in nearby Broadclyst, The New Inn serves pub grub including fish and chips and burgers (01392 461312, EX5 3BX)
EASIER ACCESS: the first swim spot is a short, flat walk of less than 5 minutes from the car park, and it is easy to walk into the water
NEARBY SWIM SPOTS: You can swim in the Exe at nearby Bramford Speke, but make sure you go in from the public footpath; there have been tensions around people trespassing on private land to access the water. The beach at Budleigh Salterton on the east Devon coast is another lovely place for a dip

Killerton is a grand country estate, now owned and managed by the National Trust. Although there is a charge to go into the house and formal gardens, a large section of the perimeter is free to access; our route takes us through this, following the course of the lovely River Culm. After your walk, do consider visiting the property or the café, as the Trust is a charity and looks after many precious landscapes across the country.

From the start at Ellerhayes Bridge it's a very short walk to the first swimming spot, on a bend in the river ❷. There is a beach, and it's popular with dogs as well as humans! It's easy to access, as you can just wade in, and if you swim upstream to the right you will find a good deep stretch overhung by willows. It all feels very English and pastoral, and you half expect to bump into Ratty or Mole from *Wind in the Willows* at any moment. Swim to the left of the entry point and you find another bend, where the water is a bit shallower but where it's still fun to explore. Occasionally you might hear or see a train rumbling past; the main line to London passes nearby.

The River Culm rises in the Blackdown Hills and runs over 27 miles to join the River Exe north of Exeter. It's the Exe's biggest tributary, and the focus of an unusual long-term project called Connecting the Culm. Like many of our rivers, the Culm has suffered flooding and biodiversity loss over the years, and the project aims to tackle this and 'future-proof' the river through a range of physical measures and also, importantly, getting local people to really connect with their river and become involved in protecting it. There are several partners in the project, from local authorities to wildlife organisations and the National Trust at Killerton.

The key aims are to reduce flooding and encourage more wildlife – but, crucially, without huge man-made interventions.

The emphasis is on 'nature-based solutions' like planting trees, creating 'leaky wood dams' of tree trunks laid across small watercourses and making 'scrapes' – small depressions in the land, like tiny ponds, which temporarily store flood water.

The idea is to make the land more sponge-like, absorbing rainfall steadily throughout the year, so that rivers aren't overwhelmed in times of excessive rain. For generations farmers have drained the land to make it more productive but, as climate change increases the intensity of rainfall in extreme weather, these drains end up deluging water fast and furiously into rivers that can't cope with the onslaught. Working with nature to 'slow the flow' during high rainfall can reduce or prevent the kind of catastrophic floods that we have been seeing more often in recent years.

Some of these innovations are visible on the first section of the route, which takes you through grand parkland with fine oak trees, up and away from the river, which you can still see off to your right. You'll notice signs and diagrams explaining the work of the Connecting the Culm project between here and Columbjohn, where the National Trust is working with the West Country Rivers Trust to restore the floodplain (which we'll visit later on in the walk). You can clearly see several 'scrapes' over to the right, in the flatlands near the river. Some are round, like shallow ponds, and others are shaped into curving lines, like mini streams. The idea is that they temporarily store flood water as well as creating new habitats for wildlife, so it's hoped they will increase biodiversity as well as help reduce the risk of flooding, particularly on the nearby railway line. At the time of writing they are still quite new, with their long-term effectiveness not yet known.

The route continues along the edge of Park Wood ❸, with more views across to the river.

There are a lot of conifers here, mainly Douglas fir planted in the late 20th century following storm damage, but there are many deciduous trees along the side of the wood, which create a gradual visual transition to the more open aspect of the Culm valley alongside. Some of the oak trees here are judged to be over 350 years old, and in spring the wood is full of wild garlic and bluebells.

After about a mile of walking through the woods you emerge into a more open area ❺, before following the route alongside a copse. Through the trees you will see a rather romantic-looking abandoned house. This is Pidgeon Cottage, and just next to it is Columbjohn Chapel ❼, two small buildings that are clues to this area's past; in Tudor times there was a large Elizabethan manor house here, and this beautiful spot by the river would have been a hive of activity.

The manor of Columbjohn (which is recorded in the Domesday Book as 'Colum') was bought in 1580 by the Acland family, who built a large mansion on the site. An inventory compiled in the 1640s, when the house was still quite new, records 22 rooms including parlours, a nursery, a hall, six small chambers, two butteries and a kitchen. Out-buildings included a coach house, a brew house, a worker's hall and other domestic properties.

Today Pidgeon Cottage and Columbjohn Chapel, together with a large gatehouse arch nearby, are the only visible evidence of what must have been a vibrant and busy place. The cottage does still have its Tudor foundations, and is thought to be on the site of a dovecote in the manor house grounds. The chapel, however, is much younger; it was built in 1844 to replace an older one. It is a pleasing little building with pretty fish-scale roof tiles and a bell tower. It is usually closed, but don't worry, according to the pioneering historian of the English landscape

WG Hoskins "The interior is of no interest but the exterior and its surroundings are very attractive."

In the 17th century the manor became caught up in the events of the Civil War. It was used as a garrison by Royalist troops, but after the triumph of Oliver Cromwell it fell into Parliamentarian hands for a while, and Cromwell himself stayed here at one point. A few decades later, the family moved to nearby Killerton House, which they'd bought shortly after acquiring Columbjohn, and the house here became derelict and was demolished in the mid-18th century. The chapel survived, and the family travelled over for worship every Sunday; they were still using it a hundred years later, when the present chapel was built.

As you walk away from the chapel you will see a large gatehouse arch over to your left. This is the only visible survivor of the Tudor buildings, dating back to the 16th century, and today serves as the entrance to a nearby farm. The route heads over to the right of the arch and into the lane, where you soon reach Columbjohn Bridge. This graceful stone structure is about 400 years old, and as you cross it you will see a large post on the right, which is there to monitor flood levels; alarmingly it goes up to nearly 2 metres above the road! A sure sign of the flooding that blights this part of the world.

There's a parking area and picnic spot **8**, and the river splits around a little island which is rather pretty. It's a fun place for another swim, although it is more of a plunge here than at the first swim spot, and from the water you get a lovely view of the bridge, which you don't see from the road.

After a swim and a pitstop, you head back past Columbjohn Chapel and to the edge of Columbjohn Wood **5**. At this point, instead of continuing back on the route you came, you bear right into the wood, to head back in a loop. The path ascends through the woods and shortly after you come across a rather intriguing sign on the right saying 'Lost House' **9**. Although there's not much to see apart from a depression in the ground, this is believed to be the site of a lost mansion, started by Sir Thomas Dyke Acland in 1775. The architect's drawings, which survive today, show a vast building, three times the size of the present-day Killerton house, in the classical style with pillars, porticos and pediments.

However, the building was never finished and the site was abandoned. As the centuries passed, its location was forgotten, although there were always rumours about it. Then a few years ago, in 2016, an archeological survey of the estate, using LIDAR (light imaging detection and ranging), showed shapes in the ground that matched the plans of the original building. It's thought the earth banks and the hollow that are visible today could be the cellars. Why the massive building project was never completed remains a mystery; one sad speculation is that the death of Sir Thomas Dyke Acland's son John, at the young age of 32, was so devastating that he gave up on the scheme.

The walk continues uphill through the woods before bearing left, at which point you start to descend into Deodar Glen **10**, its graceful cedar trees making a marked contrast to the native woodland experienced on most of the walk so far. The glen was designed in the 19th century, with the aim of recreating an alpine or Himalayan valley; such ideas were fashionable at the time, when Victorian plant collectors who had seen strange and beautiful new environments abroad wanted to recreate them at home.

The final part of the walk is an easy descent back down to Ellerhayes Bridge, where you can have another quick dip if you fancy. Do try and make time after the walk to go and look at the main house and gardens, which are spectacular.

1 Go through the gate out of the car park and bear right following the river on your right.
0.1 miles

2 You reach a bend in the river where there is a gate in the fence. This is the first swim spot. Have a dip and retrace your steps towards the car park. Once nearly back at the car park, turn right, away from the road, and pick up the track following the National Trust riding and biking sign. Follow the track west along the edge of the wood, keeping right and ignoring a path to the left.
0.8 miles

3 You reach a large fork. Go left here, taking the track uphill, following the buggy sign. The route continues uphill and then downhill again.
0.3 miles

4 You reach another fork. Bear right here, continuing downhill and following the yellow arrow and 'no buggies' sign. You reach a pair of gates. Go through and turn left, following the sign for Columbjohn Chapel and Bridge.
0.4 miles

5 You come out of the wood to a clearing with a track to the left and fields ahead. Go straight on here, walking with the field on your left.
0.2 miles

6 Turn right following the footpath for Columbjohn Chapel.
0.1 miles

7 You reach Columbjohn Chapel. After a look around, continue along the public footpath, which crosses the field diagonally to the right on a route between fences. At the road, turn right and then cross the bridge.
0.2miles

8 You arrive at the next swim spot, by the bridge. After a dip, retrace your steps, passing the chapel and returning to the edge of the wood (point 5). Here, go through the wooden gate back into the wood, walking uphill.
0.8 miles

9 You pass the site of the Lost House with an information board. Keep going uphill, ignoring paths downhill to the left.
0.3 miles

10 You reach a junction of paths with a wooden gate to the right. Do not go through the gate, but keep straight on following the sign

for Deodar Glen, walking along the edge of the woods. Bear left, crossing a dip, still following signs for Deodar Glen, then follow the path downhill in the glen.
0.3 miles

11 By the bench in the glen, keep following the path as it zig-zags down to the left. At this point there are various you can walk back to the car park, and it doesn't matter particularly which you take. We followed the path forking right, then left, following signs for Ellerhayes Bridge and Park Wood.
0.5 miles

12 You arrive at the edge of the wood. Go through a five-bar gate signposted 'Deer Park' but turn immediately left down a steep, rough path alongside the wood on your left. Go downhill until you reach a gate on your left. Turn right here and head back down to the car park.
0.2 miles

Walk 27

EXETER AND THE RIVER EXE

A fascinating and picturesque circular city walk exploring the social history of the River Exe and visiting some unexpected green spaces and a surprising number of swim spots.

Today's walk starts outside the Custom House ❶ on Exeter's historic quayside. While the quay has existed since Roman times, the construction of the nearby Exeter Ship Canal in the 1560s led to a significant increase in trade, most notably in woollen cloth. This magnificent building with Renaissance-inspired façade is thought to be the oldest brick building still standing in the city. Dating back to 1680, it is also believed to be the first purpose-built custom house in England and was run by HM Customs right up until 1989.

Today it is managed by the Exeter Canal and Quay Trust and operates as a centre for arts and culture and an interpretation centre for the waterfront area. It's free to enter, and you can watch a short film about the history of the quayside area. The unspoilt charm of the quayside area saw it standing in for Liverpool Docks in the epic 1970s television series *The Onedin Line*, and scenes were recreated shot-for-shot here in a community film project in 2023.

From the Custom House, the walk heads towards the River Exe, which we will be following for nearly all of today's route. You pass some historic harbourside buildings, including a bar called Puerto Lounge, which was once a bonded warehouse of Kennaway and Co. wine and spirit merchant and still has a cargo winch. Once by the river, the route passes under first Exe Bridge South and then Exe Bridge North, which are part of a huge roundabout called Exe Bridges. This section of river is fantastic for bird spotting, and we saw ducks, swans, geese, herons and moorhens as we followed the path.

Once you've emerged from under the two bridges, you reach an area called Exe Island and then walk up through Bonhay Meadows ❷. Much of this area is made up of student accommodation for

Exeter University, which is up on the hill above. The route heads north along the main road for a very short distance until reaching the Mill on the Exe pub, with its delightful position looking over the river. Until 1967 a paper mill stood here, but it was demolished to build the pub in 1982; the original waterwheel that was used to power the machinery can still be seen in the beer garden.

The walk then turns left past Blackaller Weir and over a striking foot and cycle bridge called Miller's Crossing, built in 2002. This has two sections, one over the river and one over the flood channel, and the first is a suspension bridge with a huge weight resembling a pair of mill stones anchoring the cables. This references the many mills that lined the leats along this part of Exeter in the past, as does the name, which was chosen in a public competition.

Once over the first bridge, you turn right at the enormous millstones and walk along Black-aller Island, which is a thin piece of land with the Exwick Flood Channel on the left and the

River Exe on the right, which is deep and wide here and perfect for swimming. After a couple of minutes' walk, you should find the first swim spot in a clearing amongst the trees ❸. Look out for a large, distinctive holm oak on the bank. There is a lovely wide section of river to swim in, backed onto by houses on the opposite side. You can swim hundreds of metres upstream, as far as the railway bridge and beyond, and it's no surprise to learn that a swimming club once operated in this area.

Head Weir Bathing Place opened in 1864 on the land opposite (now private), run by a superintendent called Frank Shooter, and remained active up until the 1940s. It started at a time when bathing was unregulated and drownings were common, so the City Council rightly felt that a dedicated swimming facility would make things much safer. By 1877 there were 15 bathing huts on a tarmac area with wooden platforms for swimmers to enter the water. Swimming matches were common, as well as displays of stunt diving and swimming. Shooter and his family would put on displays and he even had his own signature trick, diving into the water and surface with a lit cigar in his mouth. Frank became known as the 'Hero of the Exe' and was given awards for teaching thousands of people to swim and preventing 200 from drowning; apparently there wasn't one fatality in the whole 16 years that Frank was overseeing the facility. His daring rescues even inspired a pun-filled 1886 poem, found by the Life Saving Awards Research Society, which featured in a publication called Bird's Eye.

Frank Shooter is a plucky man,
As ever you should see:
To further paint him in a *Word*,
You've got to drop the *p*.
In all the risks his "pluck" has dared

His "luck" but *followed suit*;
Whenever we've required a *trump*,
He had a heart to – do't
When'er he knows a fellows *down*,
By cruel fate has *sank* –
Our Shooter's *sterling* aid is given,
and he's taken to the *bank*.
Being *under water* for a time,
Over draught you may expect;
And life which has been ebbing fast
Is saved by Shooter's *check*.
The honour *Echoes* now awards
His daring but exacts;
His *portrait* shows how justly
You *countenance* his acts.
And long may his own life be spared,
Who has lengthened others' span;
For well won ease should be the fate
Of such a *saving man*.

The walk continues up the island before crossing over Station Road bridge ❹ and then back down along the flood channel. This was created following heavy rain in the autumn of 1960, which caused the River Exe to rise 2 metres in places and overflow into large areas of the city, flooding some 2500 properties. Three flood relief channels were constructed, one of which we are now walking along; it is pretty shallow and probably stagnant, so not a good swim spot. Somewhat ironically the bridge you just crossed used to be the Bueller Bridge, but that was swept away in 1974 in a flood caused by the construction of the flood defences.

While this section of the river isn't that inspiring, it is rather wonderful for joggers, walkers, cyclists and skateboarders. The walk passes some excellent green spaces and sports facilities, as well as community gardens and allotments. The area was

actually the location of the original Roman town of Isca Dumnoniorum (or simply Isca, from the Celtic uisce for water); over time Isca became Exeter. The walk then passes under the Exe Bridges again, and arrives at the south bank of Exeter Quayside.

There are several potential entry points to get in for a swim here. The first is a small set of steps ❺, just before the Cricklepit Suspension Bridge, a footbridge that opened in 1988; there is another set of steps into the water just after it too. Where you swim may well depend on how busy the water is with swans, of which there are many around here.

Last time we swam here the area that was most clear of waterfowl was just after the Piazza Terracina on the right (by Rockfish). This space at the head of the canal basin is named after Exeter's twin town in Italy. You will spot Butt's Ferry, powered by a ferryman pulling the ferry along a cable stretched across the river, which can be lowered to the riverbed when a larger boat wants to pass. It gets its rather amusing name from Mr George Butt, an insurance broker who fought to keep the service

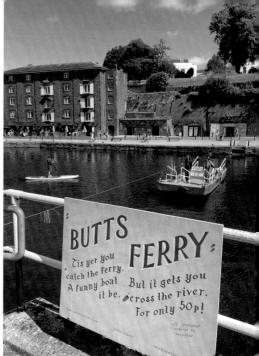

to an interesting stretch with the canal on your right and the river (with another flood channel) on your left. The Exeter Ship Canal is about 5 miles long and runs from the Exeter Canal Basin to rejoin the river beyond Exminster; when it opened in 1566, it was the first new canal in Britain since Roman times. Exeter merchants were forced to build it to restore boat access into the city after the building of impassable weirs by the local landed gentry (one of whom also built a competing port downriver), which then caused the river to silt up. The canal was busy with boat traffic for hundreds of years but has not been in commercial use since 1972. However, since then it has become of great value for leisure use, and is a very pleasant part of today's walk. The route passes over the canal via the swing bridge **6** and on towards the River Exe.

You can now either cross the river again at Trews Weir Suspension Bridge **7**, to walk back to the start, or take an optional extended spur past the allotments and into the Riverside Valley Park, an area of land between river and canal, where there is a bonus swim spot. Dubbed 'Leaf Land', it has some beautiful woodland off to the left and a few potential swim spots, although there also seem to be some fairly aggressive private fishing signs. At the end of the path, which feels like the tip of an island, you can access a bend in the river (7A) where it's lovely to swim. Do be careful if the river is in spate though. After your bonus swim, head back to the suspension bridge at point **7**. If crossing the bridge gives you wobbly legs, then it's a really pleasant walk back past the weir, where you will often spot heron fishing, then past the Port Royal Pub and back to the Exeter Custom House, with various treats and temptations awaiting the weary and thirsty walker around the quays. And of course, calories don't count after a swim.

when the council wanted to shut it down in the 1970's. It has a great sign next to it saying:

Tis yer you catch the ferry.
A funny boat it be.
But it gets you cross the river
For only 50p!

There is a small landing just after the ferry where you can get into the water, and while you will probably get some funny looks, it's completely fine to bathe here. There are great views over the old quay buildings on the other side of the river, particularly of the brick arched cellars that are home to artists and artisans and a number of other interesting businesses. In the summer months, pedalos, canoes and kayaks will also pass you on this bustling stretch of river.

The walk then continues past Haven Banks outdoor activity centre and crosses a swingbridge

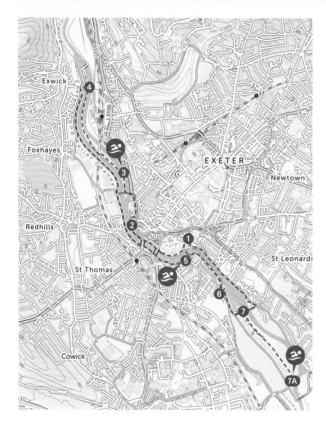

3 There is a large, spreading holm oak tree by the swim spot, which will help you to recognise it; there are other places to get in along this stretch of river but we found this one the best. After a swim, carry on walking with the river on your right. Pass under the railway bridge and continue with the flood channel on your left and the river on your right.
0.6 miles

4 At the road bridge, turn left, crossing the flood channel. At the end of the bridge turn left following the blue sign for the Exeter Cycle Route and City Centre. You're now walking with the flood channel on your left. Keep walking by the water, passing under the railway bridge and then the two road bridges with blue railings again, until you get back to the main quay area but on the other side from where you started.
1.5 miles

5 You will see a footbridge on your left. Just before here is a set of small steps where you can get into the water and have a swim. There is also another place you can get in about 150 metres on: a slipway next to the foot ferry. After, carry on walking, following the river on your left as it flows downstream.
0.3 miles

6 Cross the swing bridge left, signed 'Quay via Suspension Bridge and Riverside Park'. Continue walking with the river on your left and the canal on your right. Just past the causeway across the flood

1 With the Custom House behind you, turn right and walk past an old building on the left with 'Kennaway & Co' cut in stone at the top. Turn left just after the Kennaway building down an alleyway, following a yellow sign saying 'Canal Basin'. At the end turn right and bear right across the grassy area with the river on your left. At the far side of the grassy area pick up the concrete path alongside the river. Pass under two road bridges with blue railings.
0.5 miles

2 Shortly after passing under the second bridge, take the path to the right, away from the river, passing flats on your left. Go through a flood gate and turn left into Bonhay Road. Pass the Mill on the Exe pub on your left and then immediately turn left onto the Miller's Crossing footbridge over the river. At the enormous millstone after the first bridge turn right. Walk for about 2 minutes to find the first swim spot in the trees on the right.
0.4 miles

channel on your left, turn left across the raised bridge and follow the path as it bears right.
0.3 miles

7 You reach the Trews Weir Suspension Bridge. To loop back to the start, cross the bridge and then follow the path away from the river, past Belle Isle Park on your right. After a short distance turn left following the sign for the quay. Follow the path, with the river on your left, all the way back to the Custom House.
0.7miles

7A Alternatively, you can visit another swim spot before heading back to the start. Instead of crossing the suspension bridge, carry straight on south-east, passing the allotments and then 'Leaf Land' woodland on your left, continuing straight on until you reach the river. You feel you are on the end of a small island, as the flood channel meets the river on your right here; this is the final swim spot. If you want to make the walk more picturesque you can turn left just after the allotments through the trees; this path takes you to the river where there are other possibilities for swimming but a lot of 'fishing only' signs, before arriving at the final swim spot. To get back to the start, retrace your steps to Trews Weir Suspension Bridge **7** and follow the directions from there.

197

ABBEYFORD WOODS AND THE RIVER OKEMENT

A beautiful walk through an ancient woodland, taking in a set of mysterious old buildings as well as a swim in the gorgeous River Okement.

INFORMATION

DISTANCE: 3 miles
TIME: 3 hours
MAP: OS Explorer Map OL 113 Okehampton
START AND END POINT: Car park at Abbeyford Woods south (SX 590 963, EX20 1RJ, What3Words: fixed.provide. electrode)
PUBLIC TRANSPORT: None, although Okehampton is well served by public transport and you can use the Tarka trail to walk north-west out of the town to Abbeyford Wood (about a mile)
SWIMMING: Pool in the East Okement River (SX 595 969); there are other smaller pools along this same stretch
REFRESHMENTS: None on the walk. Dot's Café in Okehampton is a wooden cabin attached to a butchers' shop and serves pasties, pies, bacon sandwiches and cakes (01837 52114, EX20 1EU). The Fountain Inn in the centre of Okehampton is in a nice position by the river, has free wifi and accepts dogs (01837 318601, EX20 1AP)
EASIER ACCESS: Unfortunately you have to walk about 0.7 mile through the woods to reach the swim spot
NEARBY SWIM SPOTS: there is a lovely pool in the East Okement at nearby Jacobstowe. Park at the bridge over the river about 0.3 miles east of Jacobstowe on the A3072 (off the main road by the Old Mill). Cross the river and turn left along the public footpath walking with the river on your left. You will soon see a gate which leads down to a lovely pool with a cliff (SS 591 018, What3Words: nutty.ready.driveway)

Abbeyford Woods is one of 1,500 public forests across the country managed by Forestry England. The organisation has been going for over a century; it was established in 1919 as the Forestry Commission to restore the nation's woods and forests following the first world war, when cover was at an all-time low of 5%. The Forestry Act was passed to address severe timber shortages and create state-owned woods and forests, and woodland cover is now more than double what it was a century ago.

The first of many millions of trees to be planted were at Eggesford Forest, just 15 miles away from here; the young Queen Elizabeth visited Devon in 1956 to mark the millionth acre of planting. In 1964 the public was given unlimited access to the public forest estate, meaning that places like Abbeyford Woods are completely open for everyone to enjoy.

There is always something magical about being in woods, and today's walk is no exception. The forest here is primarily ancient woodland, although there are also a lot of conifers, which were planted in the early 20th century. Forestry England's plan for the wood over the next 10 years is to keep producing timber, but also to increase conservation work, "providing a forest rich in wildlife, attractive to people and increasingly resilient to climate, pests and diseases."

Setting off from the car park, you are very aware of the conifers, but they soon thin out and the woodland starts to become more diverse, with oak, birch and beech trees, and beautiful banks lined with velvety green moss. Much of the forest is a so-called 'PAW' – a planted ancient woodland site. It's one of many historic woods across the country that were planted with non-native trees to meet the urgent national need for timber in the 20th century. Between the 1930s and the early 1980s nearly half of Britain's ancient semi-natural woodlands were converted into plantations, and there is now a big emphasis on restoring these valuable habitats.

The route leaves the main path ❷, turning right and heading downhill. You will soon start to hear the river, and after a short walk you will reach it. The Okement rises on Dartmoor as two rivers: the West and the East Okement. They unite in the town of Okehampton and from here flow some way as the Okement, which eventually joins the River Torridge. The old name for the river was the Ockment, and Okehampton was known as Ocmundtune in Saxon times.

The river is swimmable from pretty much as soon as you reach it, with various pools, but access is a little difficult; the banks are quite high, although it is possible to clamber down. It's better to keep walking for a short distance with the river on your right, until you reach a beautiful clearing ❸ where there is a waterfall and a large pool with a small beach. There are a couple of swings – an old tyre and a piece of yellow plastic – hitched to the trees. Here it is easy to wade into the water for a peaceful swim, with the woods on one side and an open meadow on the other. It's also fun to climb down below the waterfall and to get a shoulder and head massage in the cascades, although take care because the bubbling water can hide rocks.

After a dip, continue to walk alongside the river until you reach a fence with a stile and a 'private' sign ❹. Needless to say, don't cross the stile, but bear left by the sign and follow the path as it heads away from the river. You'll find yourself walking through a plantation of Douglas fir trees. The atmosphere is quiet, with a soft carpet of needles underfoot which tends to muffle the noise. Although some conifer forests can feel rather sterile, this one doesn't. Moss and ferns grow below, providing a bright green contrast to the darker greens above.

You soon reach a T-junction with a track ❺ where you turn left. This feels like a very old route, which in fact it is; if you turned right, you would reach the site of an ancient priory in the riverside hamlet of Brightley. A Cistercian community was established here in 1133, but they abandoned the site after just a few years, going to Forde Abbey in Somerset instead. None of the original buildings remain, but there is a still a house called Priory Cottage, and the fact this was once a monastic site of course explains the name of Abbeyford Woods.

Turning left, you start a gradual ascent back up to the top of the woods. The path narrows, and then emerges onto a wide woodland track, where you bear right and continue uphill. The trees thin out as you get higher, and there is a more open feeling; at the top the route flattens out and there is a handily placed bench ❼ where you can take a rest. If you look south, to your left, there are great views of Dartmoor, in particular the distinctive conical shape of Steeperton Tor.

As you walk you may see signs of tree felling. Unfortunately, the wood has been affected by a disease called *Phytophthora ramorum* (meaning 'plant destroyer of branches'). There is no cure, so all that can be done is to try and slow it down by removing the infected trees. This means the place will start to look different, with new, temporary, open areas. Forestry England says this creates new habitats for insects, butterflies, moths and birds, and it will also mean that work to restore the ancient woodland advances more quickly, because the cleared areas will be replanted with young native trees to replace those that that have been felled.

The route continues to a little area of mysterious old buildings that we've dubbed 'Dystopia', in fact we call this bit of the walk the 'Dystopia Diversion' as it's a little loop that is not strictly necessary but is rather fascinating. You'll start to see some buildings on the right of the path; turn off towards them and you will come across a whole collection of strange structures, ranging from very large corrugated iron sheds to abandoned breeze block walls, and what looks like an old air raid shelter. There are patchy white road markings on what remains of a few old tarmac tracks, and some faded signs with telephone numbers that pre-date 1995, when all area codes changed to start '01'.

It seems these buildings were first erected in the forest during the second world war. According to a Government report on the history of the armed forces on Dartmoor, they were created to serve as storage depots, but no more information is given. However, villagers have told us it was actually an RAF facility; there was an RAF airfield at nearby Folly

Gate, and a NAAFI there which is now the village hall. A few years ago a memorial stone was placed in memory of the RAF presence during the war.

In the 1950s the sheds were used to store emergency supplies for use in the event of nuclear war. These days, the buildings are used by the police and fire service for training in riot and hostage situations, and it's said that one of the larger, barn-like sheds contains a replica of an actual house inside it. Groups of emergency service personnel regularly spend whole days in the forest, complete with catering, although it was quiet last time we visited. They don't prevent public access on training days.

Whatever the secret history of this rather strange collection of buildings in the middle of the forest, they certainly provide food for thought. Walking through them feels like being on some bizarre film set and is certainly memorable. After the diversion into 'Dystopia' the route continues downhill through the woods, taking you back to the car park.

DIRECTIONS

1 From the car park, with your back to the road, take the path on the right, where there is a single bar gate.
0.4 niles

2 Turn right off the main route at the first path on the right after leaving the car park, and follow it downhill. The path arrives at the river; turn left and walk with the river on your right. There are various possible swim spots as soon as you join the river, but the best is a little further along.
0.2 miles

3 You arrive at the main swim spot. It is obvious, with a large clearing and a waterfall. Stop here for a dip and then carry on walking with the river on your right.
0.1 miles

4 At a stile into a field with a 'private property no access' sign turn left, following the path into a conifer wood.
0.2 miles

5 You arrive at a T-junction of paths at the edge of the wood. Turn left here and follow the path as it starts to ascend. Ignore small paths to right and left as the path narrows and becomes stony, continuing uphill.
0.1 miles

6 The path joins a wide track. Turn right onto the track and continue walking uphill. The track flattens out for a short while and then bears right (ignore a small

path to the left). The route starts to ascend again.
0.4 miles

7 You reach an open area where there is a large pile of logs and another track off to the left. Ignore the track to the left and keep going straight, passing a bench on your right and then another track on the left. Keep going straight and you will start to see disused buildings on your right.
0.3 miles

8 Turn right off the path to explore the ruins. You can make a small circuit around them, and then come back to point 8 and retrace your steps back along the path for about 120 metres.
0.3 miles

9 Turn right off the path following a track into the woods. After about 5 minutes you reach a

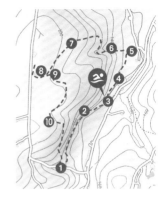

fork; bear right here down a path which soon enters pine woods.
0.4 miles

10 You reach a rather indistinct fork; bear left here and walk downhill. The path soon joins a wide track, where you turn right and follow the track back to the car park.
0.4 miles

Copyright

Editor:
Candida Frith-Macdonald
Cover illustration:
James Lewis
Design and layout:
Amy Bolt
Proofreading:
Bethany Williams
Mapping powered by:

cycle.travel

Published by:
Wild Things Publishing Ltd
Bath, BA2 7WG,
United Kingdom
wildthingspublishing.com

Acknowledgements

We'd like to thank the generous community of wild swimmers who helped us with the book. Our particular thanks are due to Debbie Travers, Jamie Turnbull, Andrew Wilsdon and Dominic Acland who shared their extensive local knowledge, and Catherine Rees-Stephan and Ron Kahana who took some amazing pictures. Thank you also to Ruth Maile and Patsy Ions who shared their knowledge about Abbeyford Woods, and Robin Franklin for his memories of Damage Farm. Lots of people helped us by testing out the wars, including, in no particular order, Rachel Dawson, Angie Watson, Judy Gordon-Jones, Symn Colwill, Yaara Lahav Gregory, Ellie Ricketts, Catherine Rees Stephan, Lara Stevens, Louise Meddemmen, Keith Meddemen, Debbie Travers, Gary Dunstan, Lynda Wilde, Lyn Cloke, Ron Kahana, Tania Goddard, Baa Goodwin, Lou Doret, Kay Pearson, Anna Dunsombe, Kathrin Deutsch, Jo Feloy, Jude Cranmer, Sally Sutton, Hilary Townsend, Janet Daley, Maria Salak, Jamie Turnbull, Judith Adams, Pauline Hall, Helen Forsyth, Melanie Scanlan, Sian Kelly, Jo London, Sam Roberts, Katie Lusty, Maureen Joyce, Rufus the Cockerpoo, and Tarka the Labradoodle. Freya Bromley, Jane Cabrera, Jane Sharkey, Linzie Freeth, Cindy Colville, Anjie Snow, Elizabeth and Harry Shatwell, Sam Roberts, Gemma Bengey, Lynsey Rowley and numerous members of the lovely Hele Bay Merbabes all answered somewhat desperate pleas for photographs when the weather or our cameras failed us. And lastly, we'd like to thank our husbands Alex and Aaron for their continued tolerance and support.

Photo credits

All images by Sophie Pierce, Matt Newbury, Aaron Kitts and Alex Murdin except inside cover flap, middle pic, Jamie Turnbull, P2-3, Dana Kahana, P13 top left Eleanor Rejzel, P19 Gemma Bengey, P21 bottom Yaara Lahav Gregory, P22 top left Maria Salak, P 26, P30 right, Ron Kahana, P46, Sam Roberts, , P73 left, Freya Bromley, P73 bottom right Jaine Swift, P75 Gemma Bengey, P79 Lucy Jones, P84 Yaara Lahav Gregory, P104 top Philip Bird, Shutterstock P121 top right Jamie Turnbull, P132 Grace Holton, P136 Ron Kahana, P147 bottom Jamie Turnbull, P153 top left, P154 top, P157, P163 top left, P165 all Catherine Rees-Stephan, P171 all Maria Salak.

Other books from Wild Things Publishing: